fitted knits

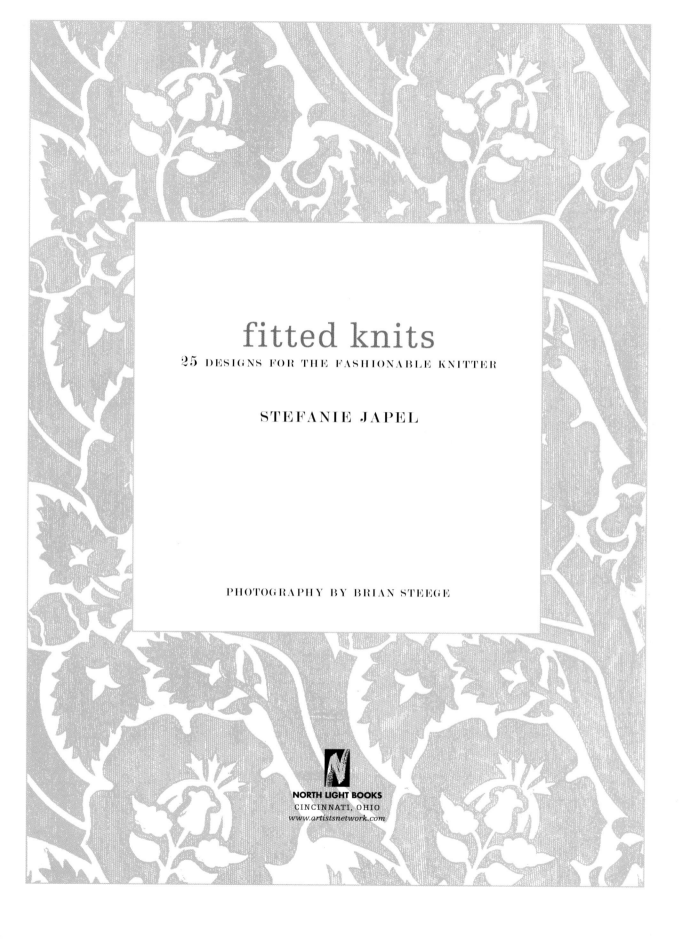

fitted knits

25 DESIGNS FOR THE FASHIONABLE KNITTER

STEFANIE JAPEL

PHOTOGRAPHY BY BRIAN STEEGE

NORTH LIGHT BOOKS
CINCINNATI, OHIO
www.artistsnetwork.com

ABOUT THE AUTHOR

Stefanie Japel has been knitting for most of her life, and she has been designing for about that long as well. Her designs have been featured on popular knitting Web sites, such as Magknits.com and Knitty.com, in the magazines *Knitscene* and *Interweave Knits*, and in books including *Stitch 'n Bitch Nation* (Workman), *Knit Wit* (Harper Collins), *Not Another Teen Knitting Book*, (Sterling), *KnitGrrl* (Watson-Guptill) and *Big Girl Knits* (Clarkson Potter). Her Web site, www.glampyre.com, receives over 14,000 hits per day. On it she posts her blog and sells original pattern designs and offers free patterns.

In her "other life," Stefanie is a geologist specializing in mineral physics. When she isn't traveling the world, she lives with her husband in Las Cruces, New Mexico.

11   10   09   08   07   5   4   3

Distributed in Canada by Fraser Direct
100 Armstrong Avenue
Georgetown, ON, Canada   L7G 5S4
Tel: (905) 877-4411

Distributed in the U.K. and Europe by David & Charles
Brunel House, Newton Abbot, Devon, TQ12 4PU, England
Tel: (+44) 1626 323200, Fax: (+44) 1626 323319
E-mail: postmaster@davidandcharles.co.uk

Distributed in Australia by Capricorn Link
P.O. Box 704, S. Windsor, NSW 2756 Australia
Tel: (02) 4577-3555

Library of Congress Cataloging-in-Publication Data

Japel, Stefanie.
   Fitted knits / Stefanie Japel. -- 1st ed.
      p. cm.
   ISBN-13: 978-1-58180-872-8
   ISBN-10: 1-58180-872-0
   1. Knitting. 2. Knitting--Patterns. 3. Sweaters. I. Title.
   TT825.J385 2007
   746.43'20432--dc22
                                      2006026201

Editor: Jessica Gordon
Art Director / Designer: Karla Baker
Photographer: Brian Steege
Stylist: Monica Skrzelowski
Make-up Artist: Cass Smith
Production Coordinator: Greg Nock
Technical Editor: Alexandra Virgiel

F+W PUBLICATIONS, INC.

ACKNOWLEDGMENTS

There are so many people to acknowledge for their help and input into this book, and I hope I don't forget anyone.

First, I'd like to thank my four handknitters, who really came through for me and who each knit beautiful garments from barely-conceived patterns: Alexandra Virgiel knit the cable-front pullover, Heather Brack knit the keyhole neckline blouse, Carie O'Cuin knit the flared-sleeved mini-sweater, and Amber Daniels-Cook knit the green coat. Thank you, ladies.

Next, I would like to thank Jean Dunbabin at Cascade Yarns for supplying the majority of the yarn used in this book. Thanks also go to Lion Brand Yarns. Melanie at Earthenwood Studio supplied all of the beautiful handmade ceramic buttons.

I would also like to thank Shannon Okey and Tricia Waddell for their support of this book in its earliest stages; Jeanie for supplying yarns "to play with" during conception of some of the earliest projects in the book; Yahaira Ferreria and Alexandra Virgiel for endless late-night discussions about the projects, yarns and life in general; and (most importantly) my tireless editors, Christine Doyle and Jessica Gordon.

Last, I thank Laura MacArthur, without whom I never would have gotten into this whole knitting pattern business in the first place.

DEDICATION

This book is dedicated to my family.

To my husband, Nathan, who lives in a yarn-filled house and has never once complained about it. To my parents, Stephen and Linda Kitchel, who have the utmost faith in me and encourage me every day to "do this full time." To my parents-in-law, Marvin and Mary Japel, who are two of my biggest supporters, and my best advertisers. To my sisters, Tonya Kitchel, Kim Forsling and Margi Japel. To my brothers, Joe, Aaron and Matt Japel, and to my nephews and niece, Alex Severn and Max and Mia Japel.

All of these incredible people have put up with me knitting at dinner, in the movies, in the car, while hiking, while playing cards... and are still waiting patiently for their sweaters!

CONTENTS

FIT AND FLATTER
an introduction

My creative career began with sewing clothes for my dolls as soon as I could manipulate a needle and thread. Then, at about the age of eight, my maternal grandmother taught me to knit. Soon thereafter, I graduated to using the sewing machine, and by the time I was in high school, I was making my own clothes and altering thrift store finds. When I was in my twenties, I was a member of the all-girl punk band Period. To draw attention away from my lack of skill on the drums, I stitched up (both sewn and knit) fantastical tops and coordinated them with wildly-printed 1960s dresses for optimal impact. Several of my early knits were recently shown at the Baltimore Museum of Art in the 2004 group exhibition aptly entitled "Dark Matter."

As an adult, I knit out of a love of fashion rather than for shock value. Making clothes for myself is also a bit of a necessity. At six feet tall, it's difficult for me to find off-the-rack clothes that fit the way they should. I spend a lot of time looking at fashion magazines, and while I'd love to have a wardrobe that's fresh off the runway, my budget just doesn't allow for many splurges of the Miu Miu or Marc Jacobs variety. So I take my favorite runway components and combine them into wearable fashion-inspired knits. The designs in this book are all things that I've knit for myself and that I actually wear.

Whether you're tall or short, curvy or slender, there is no reason to settle for less than a perfect fit, especially when you're the one making the clothing. All the patterns in this book create well-fitted garments designed to accentuate your positives. You'll be surprised at how easy it is to add shaping details that mean the difference between a potato sack and a tailored look. Oftentimes, the only shaping required is a change in needle size or stitch pattern. Additional shaping techniques used in the patterns collected in this book include short rows, darts, waist and hip shaping. I've also thrown some garments into the mix that are not shaped at all.

Most of my garments are knit in one piece, from the neck down to the hem. I've been told this is a very simplistic (read: simple-minded) method of garment construction. For me, though, it's simply intuitive. At first, constructing garments in the round grew out of a fear of seaming. To avoid seaming, early on in my knitting life I researched knitting techniques and happened upon a vintage 1950s knitting pattern worked in the round from the top down, and I fell in love. While I certainly have the skill to knit sweaters with more complex construction, I choose to stick with the straightforward in-the-round construction that allows extra planning time for choosing texture and shape.

While most of the patterns in this book share the same basic construction, there is no "percentage system," and no fractions of stitches to figure out. You simply knit to your desired measurements. Shaping can be performed at the yoke, bust, waist, hips or sleeves, depending on how closely the garment should fit. In each section of the sweater, you can simply knit more or fewer decrease or increase rounds until you have reached your personal measurements. See How to Fit Your Knits on page 13 for more detailed information on how to adjust these patterns to ensure a perfect fit for your figure.

So, pick up your needles and knit a garment with a perfect fit. There is something here to keep you knitting happily the whole year through, from lightweight summer tanks and tees to shrugs, wraps and cardigans perfect for those transitional times, and, of course, warm and cozy sweaters, vests and coats to get you through the cold months. There's even a chapter dedicated to "dress-up" clothes, including a lovely dress and a tweedy suit set. Each pattern is rated by skill level so you know what level of knitting ability is required before you begin. See the Skill Level Guide on page 11 for a brief outline of the skill levels and the techniques recommended for each one. Of course, don't be afraid to learn a new stitch or technique. Every pattern contains all the information you need to successfully complete it, and there is supplemental information in the Essential Information section at the back of the book (see page 134).

SKILL LEVEL GUIDE

Each pattern in the book is rated by skill level. Patterns rated as Supereasy are the simplest and most basic. If you're a newer knitter, you might want to start with those patterns. More intermediate-level patterns are rated as Medium, and they require a few more advanced skills. The Challenge-rated patterns are the most difficult and require a bit more complicated knitting operations. Don't let the skill level rating stop you from knitting a pattern, but do be aware of what you need to know before you start. There's nothing worse than a knitting road block that stalls your project.

SUPEREASY
You must know how to cast on and off, knit and purl, do simple increases, pick up stitches, and that's about it.

MEDIUM
You must know how to do the Super-easy stuff, be willing to do bust and waist shaping, and work buttonholes.

CHALLENGE
You must know how to do the Supereasy and Medium stuff, and be willing to do more challenging techniques, such as applied i-cord, cables and lace.

HOW TO FIT YOUR KNITS

altering the patterns in this book

Altering these patterns to fit you exactly is very easy. The patterns in this book are broken down into sections: yoke, body and sleeves. Because of the top-down construction method, you can try your garment on at each stage to make sure it fits you properly.

At the end of the yoke stage, before separating the sleeves from the body, try your sweater on and make sure the sleeve holes meet at the underarm, and that the circumference of the body is right for the fit you desire.

At the end of the bust-shaping stage, either try on the garment or use a tape measure to make sure the number of bustline increases is appropriate for your actual bust measurement. You can always knit more or fewer increases. This does change your stitch count for the later sections of the pattern, but if you keep track of how many extra (or fewer) increases you knit, it's easy to make up the difference when looking at the stitch counts in later sections.

For example, if the bust decreases are two stitches increased per round, and you are doing three extra decrease rounds, you'll just need to subtract six from your stitch count when performing the hip increases later in the pattern. Remember that knitting extra rounds also adds to the length of the pattern. I usually include a few inches of "working straight" (no increases or decreases) between bust and hip shaping, so simply subtract the number of extra rounds you've knit from this number.

knowing your measurements

Knitting is wonderful for many reasons, and one of the main reasons is that it's completely possible to make a garment that fits you *exactly* how you want it to. Before casting on for any sweater, any time you knit, you should be familiar with your own measurements. Even if you know that you *always* wear a size eight in off-the-rack clothing, take the time to find out your actual bust, waist, hip and sleeve length measurements. Knowing these numbers (and they *do* change with time!) is essential to creating garments that really fit.

Each pattern in this book is sized to specific measurements rather than giving vague sizes like small, medium and large. Generally, the measurement given is the finished bust measurement. Choose the size closest to your bust measurement, making sure to figure in how closely you'd like the garment to fit. Check the schematic(s) given for each pattern to see additional measurements for each size, such as waist and hip measurements. Then make adjustments accordingly.

ANATOMY OF A SWEATER

Most of my patterns follow the same basic formula. Know your measurements and adjust each pattern accordingly. Read through Calculating Your Fit, below, for a specific example of how you can use minor calculations to adjust a pattern to fit you perfectly.

CALCULATING YOUR FIT

Adjusting a pattern to fit your measurements exactly is simple. Let's walk through the process with Jane Q. Knitter. Ms. Knitter has a rather short torso with a high waist, and she has almost no hips to speak of. She knows, of course, the first thing she must do to knit a sweater that fits is take her measurements.

Here's what she comes up with:

> BUST: 32" (81CM)
> WAIST: 28" (71CM)
> HIPS: 32" (81CM)

She chooses to knit the 34" (86cm) bust size. The actual measurements of the sweater are:

> BUST: 34" (86CM)
> WAIST: 29" (74CM)

Because the final measurement of the sweater is close to our knitter's actual bust measurement, she won't have too much work to do in sizing the sweater for that section.

She should follow the pattern instructions as written for the 34" (86cm) size until she reaches the final yoke instruction.

For her size, the pattern reads: Purl 1 row. Rep Rows 3–4 25 times more—350 sts.

We see from the stitch count in the next pattern section that there are 184 total BODY stitches on the needle. Dividing that number by our gauge yields the actual garment measurement at that point. 184 ÷ 5½ = 33½" (85cm). Adding the button band will give an additional ½" (1cm), for a total of 34" (85cm).

The desired bust measurement is 32" (81cm), so the knitter simply needs to knit fewer raglan increases. Each round of increases adds four total body stitches, or ¾" (2cm). (There are 5½ sts in 1" [3cm].)

We know how many increase rounds it takes to get 33½" (85cm) (Row 1, Row 3, plus 25 more = 27), so we just need to calculate how many fewer increase rounds it takes to get approximately 31½" (80cm).

26 INC RNDS =
180 STS ÷ 5½ STS PER INCH = 32¾" (83CM)

25 INC RNDS =
176 STS ÷ 5½ STS PER INCH = 32" (81CM)

24 INC RNDS =
172 STS ÷ 5½ STS PER INCH = 31¼" (79CM)

Because our knitter desires a close fit, but not one that pulls across the bust, she will do 25 total increase rounds, repeating Rows 3–4 only 23 times more, for a total of 334 stitches, and 172 body stitches.

Now, she moves on to separate sleeves from the body. Because she worked two fewer increase rounds, she knows that each section will have two fewer stitches than the numbers given in the pattern.

Next comes the body section. If our knitter is short-waisted, she may wish to knit fewer than 17 rows here. She can measure her actual shoulder-to-waist length, and compare that to her garment. She knows that the row gauge is 30 rows = 4" (10cm), so there are 7½ rows in 1" (3cm). If she needs to shorten the sweater's body length by one inch, she will work seven or eight fewer body rows.

The last section she has to worry about is the waist-shaping section. Our knitter currently has 172 stitches on the needle. The numbers given in the pattern are for 184 stitches. As when separating the sleeves, because she performed two fewer increase rounds, she knows that she has two fewer stitches in each section than the numbers given in the pattern.

So, she will work the waist-shaping set up row as follows:

Knit 22, place marker, knit 42, place marker, knit 46, place marker, knit 42, place marker, knit 22. Row one of the waist-shaping section decreases two stitches at each marker, for a total of eight stitches decreased. Our knitter has a total of 164 stitches (164 ÷ 5½ = 30" [76cm]). Row 5 only decreases four stitches (160 stitches ÷ 5½ = 29" [74cm]). Row 9 decreases by eight stitches again (152 stitches ÷ 5½ = 28" [71cm]). With ½" (1cm) for the button band, this stitch count yields our knitter's desired waist measurement.

At this point, she should stop working waist decreases. Because she stopped after row 9, and the pattern continues to row 13, she should actually work 11 rows even, rather than the 7 as given in the pattern.

When starting the peplum (flared section below the waist), our knitter should be careful because the final section of the sweater is worked in a pattern stitch, and she must be sure to have the same number of stitches in the final section as the 34" (86cm) size for the stitch pattern numbers to work out correctly. Before working the lace set-up row, she should work one row, increasing eight stitches evenly. Then she can continue the peplum as instructed for the smallest size.

TUBES, TANKS AND TEES

When the days lengthen and grow warm, don't put your needles down. Trade in your woolen yarns for equally luscious cotton or cotton/synthetic blend yarns that will keep you cool both while you're knitting and while you're wearing the finished garment. Sleeveless and short-sleeved tops also have the added perk of knitting up quickly. You don't have to get bogged down with making two long sleeves, so you'll finish in a flash.

The projects in this section are perfect for keeping you fashionable through the warmer months. Knit up the sexy little tube top (page 22) for your next garden party, or try the peek-a-boo lace in the tank worked with drop stitch on for size for a hot evening out on the town (page 26). There's also an everyday tee with a decorative split neckline (page 18) and a tee knit in a bulkier-weight yarn you can wear on the first surprisingly chilly nights that herald the end of summer (page 30).

SPLIT-NECKLINE
cap-sleeved tee

This sassy little tee shirt makes you feel cute and feminine. Switch it up to make this hot little number fit your style perfectly. Choose a variegated yarn in different shades, or choose two solid colors. You could make the entire tee out of one solid color, and you may choose any button closure you wish.

Cast on at the neckline and increased at four points (sleeve "seams") until the desired bustline measurement is obtained, this tee shirt is an extremely easy-to-construct knit. There's no shaping involved, and the majority of the trim is a simple folded-picot edging. The neckline slit can be worn open or closed.

finished measurements
BUST: 34 (36, 38, 40, 42, 44)" 86 (91, 97, 102, 107, 112)cm

yarn
7 (8, 8, 8, 9, 9) balls (141 yards ea) Cascade Yarns Invito Print cotton/nylon blend yarn in color 08 variegated blues and greens (MC)

1 (1, 1, 1, 2, 2) ball(s) (109 yards) Cascade Yarns Pima Tencel cotton/Tencel blend yarn in color 7013 solid turquoise (CC)

needles
size US 7 (4.5mm) 24" or 29" (60cm or 74cm) circular needle

size US 7 (4.5mm) double-pointed needles

If necessary, change needle size to obtain correct gauge.

notions
darning needle

one clasp

sewing needle and thread

gauge
19 sts and 27 rows = 4" (10cm) in St st with MC

NOTES

[ ] (repeat operation): Rep the bracketed operation the number of times indicated.

sl (slip st[s] or marker): Slip a st or sts purlwise from the left needle to the right needle. Slip a marker from the left needle to the right needle, knitting the sts before and after it as usual.

KFB (knit 1 front and back): Inc 1 st by knitting into the front and back of the next st.

k2tog (knit 2 together): Dec 1 st by knitting 2 sts tog.

yo (yarn over): Wrap working yarn around needle clockwise, and knit next st as usual. This operation creates an eyelet hole in the knitting and inc 1 st.

yoke

With MC and circular needle, cast on 88 (92, 88, 92, 96, 96) sts. Do not join.

RAGLAN SET-UP ROW (WS): p34 (36, 36, 38, 40, 40), place marker, p10 (10, 8, 8, 8, 8), place marker, p34 (36, 36, 38, 40, 40), place marker, purl to end.

RAGLAN INC ROW (RS): KFB, [knit to 1 st before marker, KFB, sl marker, KFB] 3 times, knit to last st, KFB.

NEXT ROW: Purl.

Rep the last 2 rows 10 (10, 10, 12, 12, 12) times more, then rep RS row only once more—184 (188, 184, 204, 208, 208) sts. Do not turn. Place marker and join for working in the rnd. Knit 1 rnd.

RAGLAN INC RND: [KFB, knit to 1 st before marker, KFB, sl marker] 4 times.

NEXT RND: Knit.

Rep the last 2 rnds 10 (12, 14, 13, 15, 17) times more—272 (292, 304, 316, 336, 352) sts.

separate sleeves from body

NEXT RND: Knit front sts, place next 56 (60, 62, 64, 68, 72) sts for first sleeve on scrap yarn to be worked later, knit back sts, place next 56 (60, 62, 64, 68, 72) sts for first sleeve on scrap yarn to be worked later, place marker for new beg of rnd—160 (172, 180, 188, 200, 208) sts on needle.

body

Work even until body measures 16" (41cm) from underarm. Change to CC and work 8 rnds even.

NEXT RND: [yo, k2tog] around.

Work 8 rnds even. Bind off.

sleeves

Transfer 56 (60, 62, 64, 68, 72) held sts of one sleeve to DPNs. With CC, work 5 rnds even.

NEXT RND: [yo, k2tog] around.

Work 5 rnds even. Bind off.

finishing

neckline trim

With RS facing and using CC and circular needle, pick up and knit 88 (92, 88, 92, 96, 96) sts around neck. Do not join. Work 7 rows in St st.

NEXT ROW (RS): [yo, k2tog] to end.

Work 7 rows even. Bind off.

Fold body, sleeve and neck hems to WS on eyelet rows. With yarn threaded on a darning needle, slip sts in place.

neck opening trim

With RS facing and using CC, pick up and knit 50 (50, 50, 54, 54, 54) sts around neck slit. Knit 1 row, purl 1 row, knit 1 row. Bind off.

Weave in ends. Attach clasp. Block if desired.

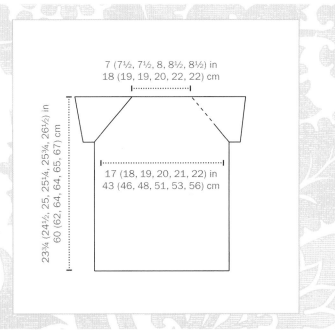

7 (7½, 7½, 8, 8½, 8½) in
18 (19, 19, 20, 22, 22) cm

23¾ (24½, 25, 25¼, 25¾, 26½) in
60 (62, 64, 64, 65, 67) cm

17 (18, 19, 20, 21, 22) in
43 (46, 48, 51, 53, 56) cm

COQUETTE LACE
tube top

Be a lawn party coquette in this basic black tube top with a demure-but-sexy twist. This simple tube is adorned with a lace panel at front center. It's perfect for hot summer days, or wear it under a blazer in cooler weather.

This pattern is an example of using simple changes in stitch pattern to shape a garment. The ribbing at the top and bottom edges provides shaping at the waist and above the bust. The insertion of a lace panel down the front center of the garment acts in place of short rows or darts, providing the same amount of "give" as trickier shaping techniques. Use Cascade Pima Tencel for next-to-the-skin softness and a subtle, curve-friendly stretch.

finished measurements
BUST: 30 (32½, 35, 37, 39½, 42, 44½)" 76 (83, 89, 94, 100, 107, 113)cm

yarn
3 (3, 4, 4, 4, 5, 5) skeins (109 yards ea) Cascade Yarns Pima Tencel cotton/tencel blend yarn in color 7779 black

needles
size US 7 (4.5mm) 24" (60cm) circular needle

size US 5 (3.75mm) 24" (60cm) circular needle

If necessary, change needle size to obtain correct gauge.

notions
stitch markers

crochet hook (optional)

ribbon or leather lacing for straps (optional)

gauge
20 sts and 28 rows = 4" (10cm) in St st

NOTES

SKP (slip, knit, pass): Sl 1 st as if to knit, k1, pass slipped st over the one just knit.

yo (yarn over): Wrap working yarn around needle clockwise, and knit next st as usual. This operation creates an eyelet hole in the knitting and inc 1 st.

k2tog (knit 2 together): Dec 1 st by knitting 2 sts tog.

k3tog (knit 3 together): Dec 2 sts by knitting 3 sts tog in the same way as for k2tog.

lace panel pattern

Lace motif is worked over 24 sts.

RND 1: SKP, k7, yo, k1, yo, p2, yo, k1, yo, k7, k3tog.

RND 2 AND ALL EVEN RNDS: k11, p2, k11.

RND 3: SKP, k6, [yo, k1] twice, p2, [k1, yo] twice, k6, k3tog.

RND 5: SKP, k5, yo, k1, yo, k2, p2, k2, yo, k1, yo, k5, k3tog.

RND 7: SKP, k4, yo, k1, yo, k3, p2, k3, yo, k1, yo, k4, k3tog.

RND 9: SKP, k3, yo, k1, yo, k4, p2, k4, yo, k1, yo, k3, k3tog.

RND 10: Rep Rnd 2.

Rep Rnds 1–10.

top ribbing

With smaller needle, cast on 150 (162, 174, 186, 198, 210, 222) sts. Place marker and join for working in the rnd, taking care not to twist sts. Work in k3, p3 rib for 13 rnds.

NEXT RND: [k1, yo, k2tog, p3] around.

Cont in k3, p3 rib for 2 rnds more. Knit 2 rnds, purl 3 rnds, knit 2 rnds, purl 3 rnds, knit 1 rnd.

body

Change to larger needle.

NEXT RND: k25 (28, 31, 34, 37, 40, 43), work lace panel patt over next 24 sts, knit to end.

Rep last row until 5 (5, 5, 6, 6, 7, 7) complete repeats of lace patt have been worked.

bottom ribbing

Change to smaller needle. Knit 1 rnd, purl 3 rnds, knit 2 rnds, purl 3 rnds, knit 1 rnd. Work in k3, p3 rib for 2 rnds.

NEXT RND: [k1, yo, k2tog, p3] around.

Cont in k3, p3 rib for 6" (15cm). Bind off loosely.

finishing

Work single crochet chains for straps, or attach ribbon or leather lacing.

Weave in ends. Block if desired.

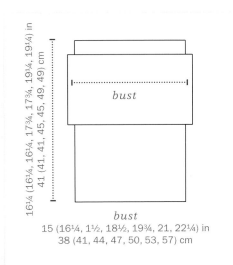

16¼ (16¼, 16¼, 17¾, 17¾, 19¼, 19¼) in
41 (41, 41, 45, 45, 49, 49) cm

bust

bust
15 (16¼, 1½, 18½, 19¾, 21, 22¼) in
38 (41, 44, 47, 50, 53, 57) cm

DROP-STITCH
lace tank

Perfect for summer, this cotton/tencel tank uses a lace stitch pattern and ribbing to create a fitted silhouette. If you've never worked a drop-stitch motif (on purpose, that is), this is a fun project for learning it. Worked at regular intervals over the tank, the teardrop-shaped dropped stitches create a peek-a-boo look that shows just enough skin.

An interesting texture turns this simple shape into a sophisticated top. It's simply constructed of two identical rectangles, with the front rectangle split at the neckline. Fasten the top button, and the neckline mirrors the shape of the drop-stitch lace motifs. Knit from Cascade Pima Tencel, this tank provides comfort and stretch.

finished measurements
BUST: 26 (28, 32, 35, 38, 40)" 66 (71, 81, 89, 97, 102)cm

This top is very stretchy. Choose a size at least 6" (15cm) smaller than your actual bust measurement.

yarn
5 (5, 6, 7, 7, 8) balls (109 yards ea) Cascade Yarns Pima Tencel cotton/tencel blend yarn in color 7013 turquoise

needles
size US 7 (4.5mm) straight needles

size US 5 (3.75mm) circular needle in any length

If necessary, change needle size to obtain correct gauge.

notions
three ½" (1cm) buttons

stitch markers

sewing needle and thread

gauge
20 sts and 26 rows = 4" (10cm) in St st on larger needles

23 sts and 26 rows = 4" (10cm) in drop-stitch lace on larger needles, unstretched

NOTES

in patt (in pattern): Cont to work in pattern as est.

yo (yarn over): Wrap working yarn around needle clockwise, and knit next st as usual. This operation creates an eyelet hole in the knitting and inc 1 st.

k2tog (knit 2 together): Dec 1 st by knitting 2 sts tog.

k3tog (knit 3 together): Dec 2 sts by knitting 3 sts tog in the same way as for k2tog.

p3tog (purl 3 together): Dec 2 sts by purling 3 sts tog in the same way as for p2tog.

drop-stitch lace

Drop-Stitch Lace motif is worked over a multiple of 8 sts + 4.

SET-UP ROW: k1, *p2, k1, yo, k1, p2, k2; rep from *, end p2, k1.

ROWS 1, 3 AND 5 (WS): p1, *k2, p2, k2, p3; rep from *, end p2, k1.

ROWS 2 AND 4 (RS): k1, *p2, k3, p2, k2; rep from *, end p2, k1.

ROW 6: k1, *p2, k1, drop the next st down to the yo, k1, p2, k1, yo, k1; rep from *, end p2, k1.

ROWS 7, 9 AND 11: p1, *k2, p3, k2, p2; rep from *, end p2, k1.

ROWS 8 AND 10: k1, *p2, k2, p2, k3; rep from *, end p2, k1.

ROW 12: k1, *p2, k1, yo, k1, p2, k1, drop the next st down to the yo, k1; rep from *, end p2, k1.

Rep Rows 1–12.

front

With larger needles, cast on 76 (84, 92, 100, 108, 116) sts. Work 19 rows (one and a half rep, including set-up row) of drop st lace pattern. Cont in k2, p2 rib for 3½ (3½, 4, 4, 4½, 4½)" 9 (9, 10, 10, 11, 11)cm more. Work 37 rows (3 rep, including set-up row) of Drop-Stitch Lace pattern.

upper left front

NEXT ROW (RS): Work 38 (42, 46, 50, 54, 58) sts in patt, place rem sts on holder.

Cont in patt on these sts until there are a total of 7.5 patt rep above ribbing. Work in k2, p2 rib for 10 rows. Bind off loosely.

upper right front

Replace held sts on needle and complete as for left side.

back

With larger needles, cast on 76 (84, 92, 100, 108, 116) sts. Work 19 rows of drop st lace pattern. Cont in k2, p2 rib until piece measures same as front to shoulder. Bind off.

finishing

neck edging

With smaller needle and RS facing, beg at shoulder, pick up and knit 3 sts for every 4 rows along split-neck edge. Place a marker at the center of the split, and place 3 additional markers evenly spaced along right front edge, for buttonholes.

ROW 1 (WS): Knit.

ROW 2 (RS): Purl, working p3tog at center marker.

ROW 3: Knit.

ROW 4: Knit, working k3tog at center marker and yo, k2tog at each buttonhole marker.

Purl 2 rows, knit 1 row, then purl 1 more row. Bind off.

Seam shoulders tog for 3 (3, 3, 3½, 3½, 3½)" 8 (8, 8, 9, 9, 9)cm on each side. Seam sides, leaving 7 (7½, 8, 8½, 8½, 9)" 18 (19, 20, 22, 22, 23)cm open for armholes.

Weave in ends. Attach buttons to align with the buttonholes on the neck edging.

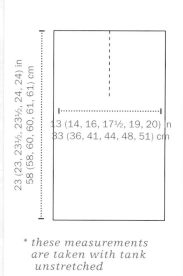

23 (23, 23½, 23½, 24, 24) in
58 (58, 60, 60, 61, 61) cm

13 (14, 16, 17½, 19, 20) in
33 (36, 41, 44, 48, 51) cm

*these measurements
are taken with tank
unstretched*

SPICY FITTED
v-neck tee

Worked in a vibrantly colored thick yarn, this tee is just the thing to layer over a blouse or a simple long-sleeved tee. Or in warmer seasons, wear it alone to show a little skin. You might even try lacing ties or ribbons through the back eyelets for a pretty, corseted look.

In this tee, the front and back of the yoke are worked separately for a few rows, then the stitches are joined to work to the hem in the round. The eyelet shaping at the front and back waist readily show off your knitting handiwork. Rows of eyelets on either side of the back shaping really define your waistline, and in front they add lots of visual interest. Neckline trim is picked up and knit after the main piece is completed.

finished measurements
BUST: 34 (36, 38, 40, 42)" 86 (91, 97, 102, 107)cm

yarn
6 (6, 7, 7, 8) skeins (109 yards ea) Cascade Yarns 109 bulky 100% wool yarn in color 0380 hot pink

needles
size US 10½ (6.5mm) 29" (74cm) circular needle

If necessary, change needle size to obtain correct gauge.

notions
stitch markers

stitch holders or scrap yarn

darning needle

gauge
12 sts and 15 rows = 4" (10cm) in St st

NOTES

sl (slip st[s]) or marker): Slip a st or sts purlwise from the left needle to the right needle. Slip a marker from the left needle to the right needle, knitting the sts before and after it as usual.

KFB (knit 1 front and back): Inc 1 st by knitting into the front and back of the next st.

SSK (slip, slip, knit): Dec 1 st by slipping 2 sts knitwise one at a time, inserting tip of left needle into both sts and knitting the 2 sts tog.

yo (yarn over): Wrap working yarn around needle clockwise, and knit next st as usual. This operation creates an eyelet hole in the knitting and inc 1 st.

k2tog (knit 2 together): Dec 1 st by knitting 2 sts tog.

RLI (right lifted increase): Inc 1 st in next st by inserting tip of right needle into back of st 1 row below on left needle and knitting into it to create a right-leaning inc.

LLI (left lifted increase): Inc 1 st in next st by inserting tip of left needle into back of st 1 row below on right needle and knitting into it.

purlwise: Perform operation indicated as if to purl (st will not twist).

WFS or WBS (work back or front straight): Work the front or the back of the garment straight with no shaping and cont in patt as est.

[ ] (repeat operation): Rep the bracketed operation the number of times indicated.

yoke

Cast on 37 (37, 43, 45, 45) sts. Do not join.

ROW 1 (WS): p6 (6, 8, 8, 8), place marker, p24 (24, 26, 28, 28), place marker, p7 (7, 9, 9, 9).

ROW 2 (RS): KFB, place marker, KFB, k3 (3, 5, 5, 5), KFB, sl marker, KFB, k22 (22, 24, 26, 26), KFB, sl marker, KFB, k3 (3, 5, 5, 5), KFB, place marker, k1, KFB—45 (45, 51, 53, 53) sts.

ROW 3: Purl.

ROW 4: KFB, [knit to marker, yo, sl marker, k1, yo] 4 times, knit to last st, KFB—55 (55, 61, 63, 63) sts.

ROW 5: sl 1 purlwise, purl to end.

ROW 6: sl 1, yo, [knit to marker, yo, sl marker, k1, yo] 4 times, knit to last st, yo, k1—65 (65, 71, 73, 73) sts.

ROW 7: sl 1 purlwise, purl to end.

Rep Rows 6–7 8 (8, 9, 9, 10) times more—145 (145, 161, 163, 173) sts.

join fronts

ROW 1: Rep Row 6 to end. At end of row, bring needles tog and join for working in the rnd. Place marker at join—155 (155, 171, 173, 183) sts.

RND 2: Knit.

RND 3: Knit to first raglan marker. Consider this the beg of the rnd. Yo, sl marker, k1, yo, [knit to next marker, yo, sl marker, k1, yo] 3 times, knit to 3 sts before center front marker, SSK, yo, k1, sl marker, k1, yo, k2tog, knit to end of rnd.

Rep Rnds 2–3 1 (2, 2, 3, 3) times more—171 (179, 195, 205, 215) sts.

separate sleeves from body

RND 1: Place next 34 (36, 40, 42, 44) sts for first sleeve on scrap yarn to be worked later, place marker for right side (RSM), k51 (53, 57, 61, 63) back sts, place next 34 (36, 40, 42, 44) sts for second sleeve on scrap yarn to be worked later, place marker for left side (LSM), k52 (54, 58, 60, 64) front sts—103 (107, 115, 121, 127) sts on needle.

body

Work front straight (WFS) to Rnd 19, working the front from marker to marker with no inc or dec, working the center front yarn over details every other row as est. Work back straight (WBS) where indicated, working the back from marker to marker with no shaping inc or dec, working the 2 lines of yarn over details every other row as est.

RND 2: WFS, k25 (26, 28, 30, 31), tie a short piece of contrast-color yarn around the 26th (27th, 29th, 31st, 32nd) (center back) st, k25 (26, 28, 30, 31).

RND 3 AND ALL ODD RNDS: Knit.

RND 4: WFS, k11 (14, 16, 15, 16), SSK, yo, k2tog, k10 (10, 10, 11, 11), knit center st, k10 (10, 10, 11, 11), SSK, yo, k2tog, knit to end—101 (105, 113, 119, 125) sts.

RND 6: WFS, k10 (11, 13, 14, 15), SSK, yo, k1, yo, k2tog, k7 (7, 7, 8, 8), SSK, k1, k2tog, k7 (7, 7, 8, 8), SSK, yo, k1, yo, k2tog, knit to end.

RNDS 8 AND 10: WFS, WBS.

RND 12: WFS, k10 (11, 13, 14, 15), SSK, yo, k1, yo, k2tog, k6 (6, 6, 7, 7), SSK, k1, k2tog, k6 (6, 6, 7, 7), SSK, yo, k1, yo, k2tog, knit to end.

RND 14: WFS, WBS.

RND 16: WFS, WBS.

RND 18: WFS, k10 (11, 13, 14, 15), SSK, yo, k1, yo, k2tog, k5 (5, 5, 6, 6), SSK, k1, k2tog, k5 (5, 5, 6, 6), SSK, yo, k1, yo, k2tog, knit to end.

front waist shaping

Front waist shaping is worked on the same rnds as the front center openwork detail.

RND 20: k11 (12, 13, 13, 14), SSK, place marker, knit to 3 sts before center front marker, SSK, yo, k1, sl marker, k1, yo, k2tog, k10 (10, 11, 12, 13), k2tog, place marker, k11 (12, 13, 13, 14). WBS—99 (103, 111, 117, 123) sts.

RND 22: Knit to 2 sts before marker, SSK, sl marker, knit to 3 sts before center front marker, SSK, yo, k1, sl marker, k1, yo, k2tog, knit to next marker, sl marker, k2tog. WBS—97 (101, 109, 115, 121) sts.

RND 24: Knit to 2 sts before marker, SSK, sl marker, knit to 3 sts before center front marker, SSK, yo, k1, sl marker, k1, yo, k2tog, knit to next marker, sl marker, k2tog, knit to LSM, k10 (11, 13, 14, 15), SSK, yo, k1, yo, k2tog, k4 (4, 4, 5, 5), SSK, k1, k2tog, k4 (4, 4, 5, 5), SSK, yo, k1, yo, k2tog, knit to end—95 (99, 107, 113, 119) sts.

RND 26: Rep Rnd 2—93 (97, 105, 111, 117) sts.

RND 28: WFS, WBS.

RND 30: WFS, k10 (11, 13, 14, 15), SSK, yo, k1, yo, k2tog, k3 (3, 3, 4, 4), SSK, k1, k2tog, k3 (3, 3, 4, 4), SSK, yo, k1, yo, k2tog, knit to end—91 (95, 103, 109, 115) sts.

RNDS 32 AND 34: WFS, WBS.

RND 36: WFS, k10 (11, 13, 14, 15), SSK, yo, k1, yo, k2tog, k2 (2, 2, 3, 3), SSK, k1, k2tog, k2 (2, 2, 3, 3), SSK, yo, k1, yo, k2tog, knit to end—89 (93, 101, 107, 113) sts.

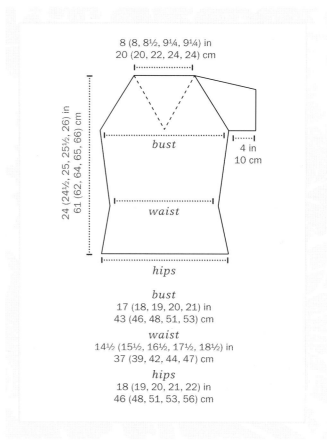

8 (8, 8½, 9¼, 9¼) in
20 (20, 22, 24, 24) cm

24 (24½, 25, 25½, 26) in
61 (62, 64, 65, 66) cm

bust

4 in
10 cm

waist

hips

bust
17 (18, 19, 20, 21) in
43 (46, 48, 51, 53) cm

waist
14½ (15½, 16½, 17½, 18½) in
37 (39, 42, 44, 47) cm

hips
18 (19, 20, 21, 22) in
46 (48, 51, 53, 56) cm

RNDS 38 AND 40: WFS, WBS.

RND 42: WFS, k10 (11, 13, 14, 15), SSK, yo, k1, yo, k2tog, k1 (1, 1, 2, 2), SSK, k1, k2tog, k1 (1, 1, 2, 2), SSK, yo, k1, yo, k2tog, knit to end—87 (91, 99, 105, 111) sts.

hip shaping

RND 44: Knit to marker, LLI, sl marker, knit to 3 sts before center front marker, SSK, yo, k1, sl marker, k1, yo, k2tog, knit to next marker, sl marker, RLI, knit to LSM, k10 (11, 13, 14, 15), SSK, yo, k1, yo, k2tog, knit to 1 st before center back st, RLI, knit center back st, LLI, k2 (2, 2, 3, 3), SSK, yo, k1, yo, k2tog, knit to end—91 (95, 103, 109, 115) sts.

RND 46: WFS, WBS.

RND 48: Knit to marker, LLI, sl marker, knit to 3 sts before center front marker, SSK, yo, k1, sl marker, k1, yo, k2tog, knit to next marker, sl marker, RLI, knit to LSM, k10 (11, 13, 14, 15), SSK, yo, k1, yo, k2tog, knit to 1 st before center back st, RLI, knit center back st, LLI, k3 (3, 3, 4, 4), SSK, yo, k1, yo, k2tog, knit to end—95 (99, 107, 113, 119) sts.

RND 50: WFS, WBS.

RND 52: Knit to marker, LLI, sl marker, knit to 3 sts before center front marker, SSK, yo, k1, sl marker, k1, yo, k2tog, knit to next marker, sl marker, RLI, knit to LSM, k10 (11, 13, 14, 15), SSK, yo, k1, yo, k2tog, knit to 1 st before center back st, RLI, knit center back st, LLI, k4 (4, 4, 5, 5), SSK, yo, k1, yo, k2tog, knit to end—99 (103, 111, 117, 123) sts.

RND 54: WFS, WBS.

RND 56: Knit to marker, LLI, sl marker, knit to 3 sts before center front marker, SSK, yo, k1, sl marker, k1, yo, k2tog, knit to next marker, sl marker, RLI, knit to LSM, k10 (11, 13, 14, 15), SSK, yo, k1, yo, k2tog, knit to 1 st before center back st, RLI, knit center back st, LLI, k5 (5, 5, 6, 6), SSK, yo, k1, yo, k2tog, knit to end—103 (107, 115, 121, 127) sts.

RND 58: WFS, WBS.

RND 60: Knit to marker, LLI, sl marker, knit to 3 sts before center front marker, SSK, yo, k1, sl marker, k1, yo, k2tog, knit to next marker, sl marker, RLI, knit to LSM, k10 (11, 13, 14, 15), SSK, yo, k1, yo, k2tog, knit to 1 st before center back st, RLI, knit center back st, LLI, k6 (6, 6, 7, 7), SSK, yo, k1, yo, k2tog, knit to end—107 (111, 119, 125, 131) sts.

RNDS 62, 64 AND 66: WFS, WBS.

Work 6 rnds garter st. Bind off loosely.

sleeves

Transfer 34 (36, 40, 42, 44) held sts of one sleeve to needle. Do not join.

ROW 1 (WS): Purl, picking up 2 sts at underarm to close the hole created when sleeves were separated from body—36 (38, 42, 44, 46) sts.

ROW 2: k16 (17, 19, 20, 21), SSK, yo, k2tog, k16 (17, 19, 20, 21)—35 (37, 41, 43, 45) sts.

ROW 3 AND ALL WS ROWS: Purl.

ROW 4: k15 (16, 18, 19, 20), SSK, yo, k1, yo, k2tog, knit to end.

ROWS 6 AND 8: Rep Row 4.

ROW 10: k15 (16, 18, 19, 20), SSK, yo, knit to end.

Work in garter st for 5 rows. Bind off loosely.

finishing

neck edging

With RS facing, pick up and knit 1 st in every st around neck. Work 5 rnds garter st, beg with a purl rnd. Bind off.

Seam sleeves. Weave in ends. Block if desired.

CRISP RECTANGLE
tunic top

Who says you have to knit from the top or the bottom to get beautiful results? Just by changing the direction of your knitting you can add a sense of freshness to your projects. The garter rows in this side-to-side knit create flattering vertical lines that complement the long and lean shape of this tunic top.

This tee is knit from side to side, using short rows to shape the hips and the neckline. Buttons at the shoulder can be buttoned or not, allowing the top to hang asymmetrically off of one shoulder. To recreate this stitch pattern, simply work a random series of knits and purls, "Morse Code" style. This piece is knit from Cascade Pima Tencel for warm-weather comfort and a beautiful hand.

finished measurements
BUST: 36 (38, 40, 42, 44, 46)" 91 (97, 102, 107, 112, 117)cm

LENGTH: 21 (24, 27)" 53 (61, 69)cm

yarn
6 (6, 7, 7, 8, 8) skeins (109 yards ea) Cascade Yarns Pima Tencel cotton/tencel blend yarn in color 8374 apple green

Yarn amounts given are enough for the long length in each size.

needles
size US 7 (4.5mm) straight or circular needles

size US 4 (3.5mm) straight or circular needles

If necessary, change needle size to obtain correct gauge.

notions
six ¾" (2cm) round buttons

sewing needle and thread to match yarn

darning needle

gauge
18 sts and 28 rows = 4" (10cm) in stitch pattern on larger needles

NOTES

wrap and turn: Bring yarn to front of work, sl next st, bring yarn to back of work, turn, slip first st, cont as given in patt.

k2tog (knit 2 together): Dec 1 st by knitting 2 sts tog.

p2tog (purl 2 together): Dec 1 st by purling 2 sts tog.

yo (yarn over): Wrap working yarn around needle clockwise, and knit next st as usual. This operation creates an eyelet hole in the knitting and inc 1 st.

seed st (seed stitch): Knit the purl sts and purl the knit sts.

stitch pattern

Work a random series of knits and purls. Some rows are entirely knit or purled, while others are worked like dashed lines, and yet others are worked in a series of Morse Code dashes and dots.

front

With larger needles, cast on 76 (90, 104) sts.

first half

ROWS 1–6 AND ALL ROWS NOT OTHERWISE SPECIFIED: Work back and forth over all sts, randomly alternating knit and purl stripes.

ROW 7 (WS) (FIRST HIP SHORT ROW): Work 30 sts, wrap and turn, work to end.

ROW 13 (SECOND HIP SHORT ROW): Work 25 sts, wrap and turn, work to end.

ROW 16 (RS) (FIRST NECKLINE SHORT ROW): Work 10 sts, wrap and turn, work to end.

ROW 21 (THIRD HIP SHORT ROW): Work 20 sts, sl next st, wrap and turn, work to end.

ROW 22 (SECOND NECKLINE SHORT ROW): Work 15 sts, wrap and turn, work to end.

ROW 27 (FOURTH HIP SHORT ROW): Work 15 sts, wrap and turn, work to end.

ROW 28 (THIRD NECKLINE SHORT ROW): Work 20 sts, wrap and turn, work to end.

ROW 32 (FOURTH NECKLINE SHORT ROW): Work 25 sts, wrap and turn, work to end.

ROW 36 (FIFTH NECKLINE SHORT ROW): Work 30 sts, wrap and turn, work to end.

ROW 40 (SIXTH NECKLINE SHORT ROW): Work 35 sts, wrap and turn, work to end.

ROW 46 (SEVENTH NECKLINE SHORT ROW): Work 40 sts, wrap and turn, work to end.

ROW 50 (EIGHTH NECKLINE SHORT ROW): Work 45 sts, wrap and turn, work to end.

ROW 54 (NINTH NECKLINE SHORT ROW): Work 50 sts, wrap and turn, work to end.

Work even until piece measures 10½ (11½, 12½, 13½, 14½, 15½)" 27 (29, 32, 34, 37, 39)cm from cast-on edge, measuring straight down center of work where there are no short rows. End with a WS row.

second half

ROW 1 (RS) (TENTH NECKLINE SHORT ROW): Work 50 sts, wrap and turn, work to end.

ROW 5 (11TH NECKLINE SHORT ROW): Work 45 sts, wrap and turn, work to end.

ROW 9 (12TH NECKLINE SHORT ROW): Work 40 sts, wrap and turn, work to end.

ROW 15 (13TH NECKLINE SHORT ROW): Work 35 sts, wrap and turn, work to end.

ROW 19 (14TH NECKLINE SHORT ROW): Work 30 sts, wrap and turn, work to end.

ROW 23 (15TH NECKLINE SHORT ROW): Work 25 sts, wrap and turn, work to end.

ROW 27 (16TH NECKLINE SHORT ROW): Work 20 sts, wrap and turn, work to end.

ROW 28 (5TH HIP SHORT ROW): Work 15 sts, wrap and turn, work to end.

ROW 33 (17TH NECKLINE SHORT ROW): Work 15 sts, wrap and turn, work to end.

ROW 34 (6TH HIP SHORT ROW): Work 20 sts, wrap and turn, work to end.

ROW 41 (18TH NECKLINE SHORT ROW): Work 10 sts, wrap and turn, work to end.

ROW 42 (7TH HIP SHORT ROW): Work 25 sts, wrap and turn, work to end.

ROW 48 (8TH HIP SHORT ROW): Work 30 sts, wrap and turn, work to end.

ROWS 49–54: Work even.

Bind off.

back

With larger needles, cast on 76 (90, 104) sts.

first half

ROWS 1–6 AND ALL ROWS NOT OTHERWISE SPECIFIED: Work back and forth over all sts, randomly alternating knit and purl stripes.

ROW 7 (WS) (FIRST HIP SHORT ROW): Work 30 sts, wrap and turn, work to end.

ROW 13 (SECOND HIP SHORT ROW): Work 25 sts, wrap and turn, work to end.

ROW 21 (THIRD HIP SHORT ROW): Work 20 sts, wrap and turn, work to end.

ROW 27 (FOURTH HIP SHORT ROW): Work 15 sts, wrap and turn, work to end.

Work even until piece measures 14 (15, 16, 17, 18, 19)" 36 (38, 41, 43, 46, 48)cm from cast-on edge, measuring straight down center of work where there are no short rows. End with a RS row.

second half

ROW 1 (WS) (FIFTH HIP SHORT ROW): Work 15 sts, wrap and turn, work to end.

ROW 7 (SIXTH HIP SHORT ROW): Work 20 sts, wrap and turn, work to end.

ROW 15 (SEVENTH HIP SHORT ROW): Work 25 sts, wrap and turn, work to end.

ROW 21 (EIGHTH HIP SHORT ROW): Work 30 sts, wrap and turn, work to end.

ROWS 22–27: Work even.

Bind off.

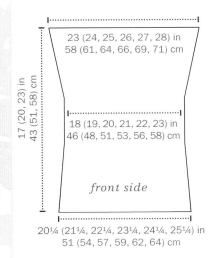

23 (24, 25, 26, 27, 28) in
58 (61, 64, 66, 69, 71) cm

17 (20, 23) in
43 (51, 58) cm

18 (19, 20, 21, 22, 23) in
46 (48, 51, 53, 56, 58) cm

front side

20¼ (21¼, 22¼, 23¼, 24¼, 25¼) in
51 (54, 57, 59, 62, 64) cm

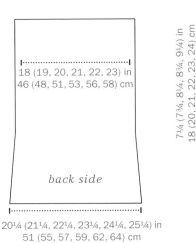

18 (19, 20, 21, 22, 23) in
46 (48, 51, 53, 56, 58) cm

back side

20¼ (21¼, 22¼, 23¼, 24¼, 25¼) in
51 (55, 57, 59, 62, 64) cm

5½ in
14 cm

7¼ (7¾, 8¼, 8¾, 9¼) in
18 (20, 21, 22, 23, 24) cm

½ sleeve

* *hem band not shown*

sleeves

With RS facing, using larger needle, pick up and knit 40 (42, 44, 46, 48) sts along left edge of front, beg at shoulder.

ROW 1 (WS): Knit.

ROW 2: Purl to last 2 sts, p2tog.

ROW 3: k2tog, knit to end.

ROW 4: Knit to last 2 sts, k2tog.

ROW 5: p2tog, purl to end.

ROW 6: Change to smaller needle. Purl to last 2 sts, p2tog.

ROW 7: k2tog, knit to end.

ROW 8: Purl to last 2 sts, p2tog.

ROW 9: k2tog, knit to end—32 (34, 36, 38, 40) sts.

ROW 10: Knit.

Work 29 rows in seed st, ending with a RS row. Purl 2 rows, knit 1 row, purl 2 rows, knit 2 rows, purl 1 row, knit 1 more row. Bind off loosely.

Rep sleeve instructions 3 times more on rem edges, reversing shaping for right front and left back edges.

finishing

hem

With RS facing and using smaller needle, pick up and knit 3 sts for every 4 rows along bottom edge of front. Knit 1 row, purl 1 row, knit 2 rows, purl 1 row, knit 1 row, then purl 2 rows. Work in seed st for 2¼" (6cm), ending with a RS row. Knit 1 row, purl 1 row, knit 2 rows, purl 2 rows, knit 1 row, purl 1 more row. Bind off loosely.

Rep for back hem.

neck edging

With RS facing and using smaller needle, pick up and knit 3 sts for every 4 rows along entire top edge of front, including sleeves. Knit 1 row, purl 1 row, knit 2 rows, purl 2 rows, knit 1 row, purl 1 row. Bind off loosely.

With RS facing and using smaller needle, pick up and knit 3 sts for every 4 rows along entire top edge of back. At each end, place 3 markers for buttonholes: one at the edge of the work, one approx 5" (13cm) in from the edge, and one approx 8 to 9" (20 to 23cm) in from the edge. Knit 1 row, purl 1 row, knit 1 row.

NEXT ROW: Knit, working [yo, k2tog] at each marker.

Purl 2 rows, knit 1 row, purl 1 row.

Sew side and sleeve seams. Attach buttons. Weave in ends. Block if desired.

SHRUGS, CARDIGANS AND WRAPS

During those transitional days between seasons, the weather can be as changeable and fickle as the "romantic" relationship between two seventh graders. One day it's blazing hot, and the next it's cooled down unexpectedly. So whether it's time to wake up again after a long sleepy winter or to brace yourself for the coming cold, it's key to have some favorite shrugs, wraps or cardigans to layer on as the weather dictates.

Knit up the little shrug featured in this chapter to keep in your locker, office drawer or bookbag to throw on over lightweight tops when the morning walks or bike rides to work or school grow cooler (page 44). Or choose the lush purple mini cardigan with long flared sleeves and a beautiful rose-shaped button (page 54), the lightweight wrap sweater (page 62), the more substantial short-sleeved ribbed cardigan (page 70), the very feminine puff-sleeved cardigan with peplum (page 66), or a lightweight short cardigan with ties ending in knitted leaves (page 58). For warmer options, knit the bulky mini cardi (page 48) or the long-sleeved Victorian cardigan with cables (page 74).

TWO-TONE
ribbed shrug

Choose your two favorite bright colors to knit this shrug. Even as the evenings grow cooler and the days shorten, you'll bring a bit of summer warmth with you into the fall. Slip this shrug on over a sleeveless top or a sundress and blur the boundaries between seasons.

This little shrug is a great introduction to raglan armhole shaping, the same concept used in all of the more complicated garments in this book. The shrug is cast on at the back neck edge and worked until the desired shoulder-to-shoulder measurement is reached. Stitches are picked up all around the neck and body edge after the back and arms are completed and worked in the round. The ribbing can either be folded or worn up as in the photo. Knit from Cascade Superwash wool, this shrug can be machine washed.

finished measurements
SHOULDER-TO-SHOULDER:
13 (14, 15, 16, 17, 18, 19, 20)"
33 (36, 38, 41, 43, 46, 48, 51)cm

Measurement is taken across the back from one shoulder to the other. If you are between sizes, make the next size down.

yarn
1 (1, 2, 2, 2, 2, 3, 3) skeins (220 yards ea) Cascade 220 Superwash 100% wool yarn in color 829 magenta (MC)

1 (1, 1, 1, 1, 2, 2, 2) skein(s) in color 814 cobalt blue (CC)

needles
size US 8 (5mm) 24" (61cm) circular needle

size US 5 (3.5mm) 24" (61cm) circular needle

If necessary, change needle size to obtain correct gauge.

notions
stitch markers

stitch holders or scrap yarn

gauge
20 sts and 26 rows = 4" (10cm) in St st with larger needle

NOTES

KFB (knit 1 front and back): Inc 1 st by knitting into the front and back of the next st.

PFB (purl 1 front and back): Inc one st by purling into the front and back of the next st.

M1P (make 1 purl): Inc 1 st by picking up the bar between the next st and the st just knit and purling it.

[ ] (repeat operation): Rep the bracketed operation the number of times indicated.

sl (slip st[s] or marker): Slip a st or sts purlwise from the left needle to the right needle. Slip a marker from the left needle to the right needle, knitting the sts before and after it as usual.

body

With larger needle and MC, cast on 43 sts. Do not join.

ROW 1 (WS): PFB, p7, place marker, p27, place marker, purl to end—44 sts.

ROW 2 (RS): KFB, [knit to 1 st before marker, KFB, sl marker, KFB] twice, knit to end—49 sts.

ROW 3: PFB, purl to end—50 sts.

Rep Rows 2–3 17 (19, 22, 24, 27, 29, 32, 34) times more, then rep Row 2 once more—157 (169, 187, 199, 217, 229, 247, 259) total sts.

NOTE: The 65 (69, 75, 79, 85, 89, 95, 99) sts in the section between the 2 markers is the lower back edge. The sts outside the markers are for the sleeves.

Place back and right sleeve sts on scrap yarn to be worked later.

left sleeve

Work even on the 46 (50, 56, 60, 66, 70, 76, 80) left sleeve sts for 24 (24, 28, 28, 28, 34, 34, 34) rows, decreasing 0 (0, 2, 2, 0, 0, 2, 2) sts evenly spaced across last row—46 (50, 54, 58, 66, 70, 74, 78) sts. Purl 1 WS row. Change to CC and smaller needle. Work in k2, p2 rib for 20 (20, 24, 24, 24, 28, 28, 28) rows. Bind off loosely.

Seam sleeve.

right sleeve

Replace right sleeve sts on needle and work as for left sleeve.

ribbing

With RS facing and beg at the back right shoulder, using the smaller needle and CC, pick up and knit sts for ribbing around the entire edge as foll:

Pick up and k27 sts along the back of the neck, pick up and k36 (40, 45, 49, 56, 60, 65, 69) sts along left front, k65 (69, 75, 79, 85, 89, 95, 99) sts from scrap yarn for lower back, pick up and k36 (40, 45, 49, 56, 60, 65, 69) sts along right front—164 (176, 192, 204, 224, 236, 252, 264) total sts. Place marker and join for working in the rnd. Work in k2, p2 rib for 14 (14, 14, 18, 18, 18, 18) rnds.

INC RND: k2, p1, M1P, p1, M1P, [k2, p2] 5 times, k2, p1, M1P, p1, M1P, [k2, p2] 7 times, k2, p1, M1P, p1, M1P, [k2, p2] to 32 sts before marker, k2, p1, M1P, p1, M1P, [k2, p2] to end of rnd—172 (184, 200, 212, 232, 244, 260, 272) sts.

Work 1 rnd in rib, keeping patt correct by working p4 in increased sections.

INC RND: k2, p1, M1P, k2, p1, M1P, [k2, p2] 5 times, k2, p1, M1P, k2, p1, M1P, [k2, p2] 7 times, k2, p1, M1P, k2, p1, M1P, [k2, p2] to 34 sts before marker, k2, p1, M1P, k2, p1, M1P, [k2, p2] to end of rnd—180 (192, 208, 220, 240, 252, 268, 280) sts.

Work 6 rnds in k2, p2 rib as est.

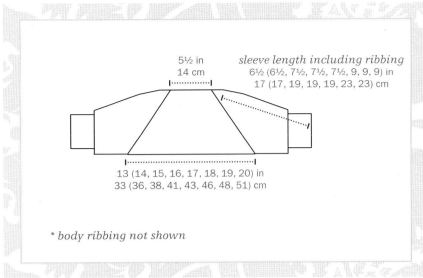

5½ in
14 cm

sleeve length including ribbing
6½ (6½, 7½, 7½, 7½, 9, 9, 9) in
17 (17, 19, 19, 19, 23, 23) cm

13 (14, 15, 16, 17, 18, 19, 20) in
33 (36, 38, 41, 43, 46, 48, 51) cm

* *body ribbing not shown*

INC RND: [k2, p1, M1P, p1, M1P] twice, [k2, p2] 5 times, [k2, p1, M1P, p1, M1P] twice, [k2, p2] 7 times, [k2, p1, M1P, p1, M1P) twice, [k2, p2] to 36 sts before marker, [k2, p1, M1P, p1, M1P), twice, [k2, p2] to end of rnd.

Work 1 rnd in rib, keeping patt correct by working p4 in increased sections.

INC RND: k2, [p1, M1P, k2] 3 times, p1, M1P, [k2, p2] 5 times, k2, [p1, M1P, k2] 3 times, p1, M1P, [k2, p2] 7 times, k2, [p1, M1P, k2] 3 times, p1, M1P, [k2, p2] to 40 sts before marker, k2, [p1, M1P, k2] 3 times, p1, M1P, [k2, p2] to end of rnd.

Work 6 rnds in k2, p2 rib as est. Bind off loosely.

finishing

Weave in ends. Block if desired.

BOLD AND BULKY
mini cardi

The boldly contrasting borders, patterned sleeve "seams" and gigantic buttons add visual interest and a mod sensibility to this mini cardigan. Worn open, the sweater takes on a bolero-style shape. Make this pattern your own by choosing the colors that suit you best. Perhaps you'd like to knit it in monochromatic shades with matching buttons instead of in contrasting colors. Or choose a third high-contrast color for the buttons if you're all about brights.

Worked with bulky yarn on large needles, this cardigan is a high-speed knit. Bust and back darts create a tailored fit, and the sleeves are shaped at both shoulder and elbow. Knit from Lion Brand Wool-Ease Thick & Quick, it's fast and affordable to make.

finished measurements
BUST: 38 (44, 49, 55)"
97 (112, 125, 140)cm

Sizes are given as S (M, L, XL) in pattern.

yarn
2 (3, 3, 4) skeins (106 yards ea) Lion Brand Wool-Ease Thick & Quick acrylic/wool blend superbulky yarn in color 170 blue (MC)

1 skein in color 131 green (CC)

needles
size US 13 (9mm) 24" or 29" (61 or 74cm) circular needle

size US 10½ (6.5mm) straight or circular needle(s)

size US 9 (5.5mm) circular needle in any length

If necessary, change needle size to obtain correct gauge.

notions
stitch markers

stitch holders or scrap yarn

darning needle

three 2" (5cm) buttons

sewing needle and thread

gauge
8 sts and 13 rows = 4" (10cm) in St st on largest needles

NOTES

KFB (knit 1 front and back): Inc 1 st by knitting into the front and back of the next st.

PFB (purl 1 front and back): Inc one st by purling into the front and back of the next st.

M1P (make 1 purl): Inc 1 st by picking up the bar between the next st and the st just knit and purling it.

[ ] (repeat operation): Rep the bracketed operation the number of times indicated.

sl (slip st[s] or marker): Slip a st or sts purlwise from the left needle to the right needle. Slip a marker from the left needle to the right needle, knitting the sts before and after it as usual.

work 2 tog (knit or purl 2 together): Dec 1 st by knitting or purling 2 sts tog as one, in keeping with est patt.

yo (yarn over): Wrap working yarn around needle clockwise, and knit next st as usual. This operation creates an eyelet hole in the knitting and inc 1 st.

SSK (slip, slip, knit): Dec 1 st by slipping 2 sts knitwise one at a time, inserting tip of left needle into both sts and knitting the 2 sts tog.

k2tog (knit 2 together): Dec 1 st by knitting 2 sts tog.

RLI (right lifted increase): Inc 1 st in next st by inserting tip of right needle into back of st 1 row below on left needle and knitting into it to create a right-leaning inc.

LLI (left lifted increase): Inc 1 st in next st by inserting tip of left needle into back of st 1 row below on right needle and knitting into it to create a left-leaning inc.

{ SMALL }

yoke

With MC and largest needle, cast on 30 sts.

ROW 1 (RS): k1, yo, k1, place marker, yo, k4, yo, k1, place marker, yo, k16, yo, k1, place marker, yo, k4, yo, k1, place marker, yo, k1—38 sts.

ROW 2 AND ALL WS ROWS: Purl.

ROW 3: KFB, [knit to 1 st before marker, yo, k1, sl marker, yo] 4 times, knit to last st, KFB—48 sts.

ROWS 5, 7, 9, 11 AND 13: Rep Row 3—98 sts.

ROW 15: [Knit to 1 st before marker, yo, k1, sl marker, yo] 4 times, knit to end—106 sts.

ROW 17: Rep Row 15—114 sts.

ROW 19: Knit to 1 st before marker, yo, k1, sl marker, yo, k9, SSK, k2tog, k9, yo, k1, sl marker, yo, k15, SSK, k2tog, k15, yo, k1, sl marker, yo, k9, SSK, k2tog, k9, yo, k1, sl marker, yo, knit to end—116 sts.

separate sleeves from body

ROW 20 (WS): p18, place next 22 sts for first sleeve on scrap yarn, p36, place next 22 sts for second sleeve on scrap yarn, p18—72 sts on needle.

body

ROWS 21 AND 25: Knit.

ROW 23: k34, SSK, k2tog, k34—70 sts.

ROW 27: k33, SSK, k2tog, k33—68 sts.

ROW 29: k7, SSK, k2tog, k46, SSK, k2tog, k7—64 sts.

ROW 31: k6, SSK, k2tog, k20, SSK, k2tog, k20, SSK, k2tog, k6—58 sts.

ROW 33: k5, SSK, k2tog, k40, SSK, k2tog, k5—54 sts.

ROW 35: Change to size US 10½ (6.5mm) needle and CC, knit.

ROW 36 (WS): Knit.

Purl 2 rows, then work in k2, p2 rib for 5 rows. Purl 2 rows, knit 1 row, then purl 1 more row. Bind off loosely.

{ MEDIUM }

yoke

With MC and largest needle, cast on 38 sts.

ROW 1 (RS): k1, yo, k1, place marker, k6, yo, k1, place marker, yo, k20, yo, k1, place marker, yo, k6, yo, k1, place marker, yo, k1—46 sts.

ROW 2 AND ALL WS ROWS: Purl.

ROW 3: KFB, [knit to 1 st before marker, yo, k1, sl marker, yo] 4 times, knit to last st, KFB—56 sts.

ROWS 5, 7, 9, 11, 13 AND 15: Rep Row 3—116 sts.

ROW 17: [Knit to 1 st before marker, yo, k1, sl marker, yo] 4 times, knit to end—124 sts.

ROW 19: Knit to 1 st before marker, yo, k1, sl marker, yo, k10, SSK, k2tog, k10, yo, k1, sl marker, yo, k17, SSK, k2tog, k17, yo, k1, sl marker, yo, k10, SSK, k2tog, k10, yo, k1, sl marker, yo, knit to end—126 sts.

ROW 21: Rep Row 17—134 sts.

ROW 23: Knit to 1 st before marker, yo, k1, sl marker, yo, k11, SSK, k2tog, k11, yo, k1, sl marker, yo, k18, SSK, k2tog, k18, yo, k1, sl marker, k1, yo, k11, SSK, k2tog, k11, yo, k1, sl marker, yo, knit to end—136 sts.

separate sleeves from body

ROW 24 (WS): p21, place next 26 sts for first sleeve on scrap yarn, p42, place next 26 sts for second sleeve on scrap yarn, p21—84 sts on needle.

body

ROW 25: Knit.

ROW 27: k40, SSK, k2tog, k40—82 sts.

ROW 29: k9, SSK, k2tog, k56, SSK, k2tog, k9—78 sts.

ROW 31: k8, SSK, k2tog, k25, SSK, k2tog, k25, SSK, k2tog, k8—72 sts.

ROW 33: k7, SSK, k2tog, k50, SSK, k2tog, k7—68 sts.

ROW 35: Change to size US 10½ (6.5mm) needle and CC, knit.

ROW 36 (WS): Knit.

Purl 2 rows, then work in k2, p2 rib for 5 rows. Purl 2 rows, knit 1 row, then purl 1 more row. Bind off loosely.

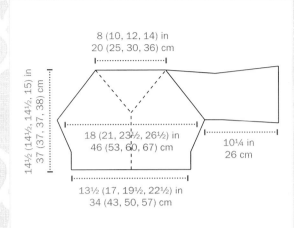

8 (10, 12, 14) in
20 (25, 30, 36) cm

14½ (14½, 14½, 15) in
37 (37, 37, 38) cm

18 (21, 23½, 26½) in
46 (53, 60, 67) cm

10¼ in
26 cm

13½ (17, 19½, 22½) in
34 (43, 50, 57) cm

* measurements do not include button bands

yoke

With MC and largest needle, cast on 46 sts.

ROW 1 (RS): k1, yo, k1, place marker, yo, k8, yo, k1, place marker, yo, k24, yo, k1, place marker, yo, k8, yo, k1 place marker, yo, k1—54 sts.

ROW 2 AND ALL WS ROWS: Purl.

ROW 3: KFB, [knit to 1 st before marker, yo, k1, sl marker, yo] 4 times, knit to last st, KFB—64 sts.

ROWS 5, 7, 9, 11, 13, 15 AND 17: Rep Row 3—134 sts.

ROW 19: KFB, knit to 1 st before marker, yo, k1, sl marker, yo, k11, SSK, k2tog, k11, yo, k1, sl marker, yo, k19, SSK, k2tog, k19, yo, k1, sl marker, yo, k11, SSK, k2tog, k11, yo, k1, sl marker, yo, knit to last st, KFB—138 sts.

ROW 21: Rep Row 3—148 sts.

ROW 23: Knit to 1 st before marker, yo, k1, sl marker, yo, k12, SSK, k2tog, k12, yo, k1, sl marker, yo, k20, SSK, k2tog, k20, yo, k1, sl marker, yo, k12, SSK, k2tog, yo, k1, sl marker, yo, knit to end—150 sts.

separate sleeves from body

ROW 24 (WS): p24, place next 28 sts for first sleeve on scrap yarn, p46, place next 28 sts for second sleeve on scrap yarn, p24—94 sts on needle.

body

ROW 25: Knit.

ROW 27: k45, SSK, k2tog, k45—92 sts.

ROW 29: k10, SSK, k2tog, k64, SSK, k2tog, k10—88 sts.

ROW 31: k9, SSK, k2tog, k29, SSK, k2tog, k29, SSK, k2tog, k9—82 sts.

ROW 33: k8, SSK, k2tog, k58, SSK, k2tog, k8—78 sts.

ROW 35: Change to size US 10½ (6.5mm) needle and CC, knit.

ROW 36 (WS): Knit.

Purl 2 rows, then work in k2, p2 rib for 5 rows. Purl 2 rows, knit 1 row, then purl 1 more row. Bind off loosely.

yoke

With MC and largest needle, cast on 54 sts.

ROW 1 (RS): k1, yo, k1, place marker, yo, k10, yo, k1, place marker, yo, k28, yo, k1, place marker, yo, k10, yo, k1, place marker, yo, k1—62 sts.

ROW 2 AND ALL WS ROWS: Purl.

ROW 3: KFB, [knit to 1 st before marker, yo, k1, sl marker, yo] 4 times, knit to last st, KFB—72 sts.

ROWS 5, 7, 9, 11, 13, 15, 17 AND 19: Rep Row 3—150 sts.

ROW 21: KFB, knit to 1 st before marker, yo, k1, sl marker, yo, k13, SSK, k2tog, k13, yo, k1, sl marker, yo, k22, SSK, k2tog, k22, yo, k1, sl marker, yo, k13, SSK, k2tog, k13, yo, k1, sl marker, yo, knit to last st, KFB—154 sts.

ROW 23: Rep Row 3—164 sts.

ROW 25: Knit to 1 st before marker, yo, k1, sl marker, yo, k14, SSK, k2tog, k14, yo, k1, sl marker, yo, k23, SSK, k2tog, k23, yo, k1, sl marker, yo, k14, SSK, k2tog, k14, yo, k1, sl marker, yo, knit to end—166 sts.

ROW 27: [Knit to 1 st before marker, yo, k1, sl marker, yo] 4 times, knit to end—174 sts.

separate sleeves from body

ROW 28 (WS): p27, place next 34 sts for first sleeve on scrap yarn, p52, place next 34 sts for second sleeve on scrap yarn, p27—106 sts on needle.

ROW 29: k51, SSK, k2tog, k51—104 sts.

ROW 31: k12, SSK, k2tog, k72, SSK, k2tog, k12—100 sts.

ROW 33: k11, SSK, k2tog, k33, SSK, k2tog, k33, SSK, k2tog, k11—94 sts.

ROW 35: k10, SSK, k2tog, k66, SSK, k2tog, k10—90 sts.

ROW 37: Change to size US 10½ (6.5mm) needle and CC, knit.

ROW 38 (WS): Knit.

Purl 2 rows, then work in k2, p2 rib for 5 rows. Purl 2 rows, knit 1 row, then purl 1 more row. Bind off loosely.

{ ALL SIZES }

sleeves

Replace 22 (26, 28, 34) held sts of one sleeve on needle. Do not join.

ROW 1 (WS): p11 (13, 14, 17), place marker, p11 (13, 14, 17).

ROW 2 (RS): Knit to 2 sts before marker, SSK, sl marker, k2tog, knit to end—20 (24, 26, 32) sts.

ROWS 3–21: Work even in St st.

ROW 22: Knit to 1 st before marker, RLI, k2, LLI, knit to end—22 (26, 28, 34) sts.

ROWS 23 AND 25: Purl.

ROWS 24 AND 26: Rep Row 20—26 (30, 32, 38) sts.

ROWS 27–29: Work even in St st.

ROW 30: Change to size US 10½ (6.5mm) needle and CC, knit.

Knit 1 row, purl 1 row, knit 1 row. Bind off loosely.

finishing

With RS facing, using size US 9 (5mm) needle and CC, pick up and knit 53 (55, 55, 57) sts along right front, 30 (38, 46, 54) sts across tops of sleeves and back neck, and 53 (55, 55, 57) sts along left front—136 (148, 156, 168) sts.

ROW 1 (WS): Knit.

ROW 2 (RS): Purl.

ROWS 3–4: Knit.

ROW 5: Purl.

ROW 6: k3 (4, 4, 5), [bind off 3 sts, k3] twice, bind off 3 sts, knit to end.

ROW 7: Purl, casting on 3 sts over each bound-off section.

ROWS 8–9: Knit.

ROW 10: Purl.

Bind off loosely. Seam sleeves. Weave in ends. Attach buttons. Block if desired.

CARIE CROPPED
flared-sleeve cardigan

Bring out your inner Jane Austen when you wear this bulky shrug. The open neckline and long, fitted sleeves say "sophisticated," while the bulky yarn and stylized increases scream "modern." Layer it over a little cotton dress or silk chemise, depending on what mood you're in…or which character you'd like to portray…good girl Jane Bennet, or bad girl Caroline Bingley.

This sweater is knit from the neckline down to the hem, with the sleeves knit flat and seamed later. Decorative yarn-over increases create a slightly flared shape for the sleeves. The sweater closes with a single ornamental button.

finished measurements
BUST: 33 (36, 38½, 41, 44)"
84 (91, 98, 104, 112)cm

yarn
2 (3, 3, 3, 3) skeins (123 yards ea) Cascade Yarns Magnum 100% wool yarn in color 9453 purple

needles
size US 15 (10mm) circular needle in any length

If necessary, change needle size to obtain correct gauge.

notions
stitch markers

stitch holders or scrap yarn

crochet hook (optional)

one 1½" (4cm) button

gauge
6 sts and 11 rows = 4" (10cm) in St st

NOTES

[ ] (repeat operation): Rep the bracketed operation the number of times indicated.

sl (slip st[s] or marker): Slip a st or sts purlwise from the left needle to the right needle. Slip a marker from the left needle to the right needle, knitting the sts before and after it as usual.

KFB (knit 1 front and back): Inc 1 st by knitting into the front and back of the next st.

SSK (slip, slip, knit): Dec 1 st by slipping 2 sts knitwise one at a time, inserting tip of left needle into both sts and knitting the 2 sts tog.

k2tog (knit 2 together): Dec 1 st by knitting 2 sts tog.

yo (yarn over): Wrap working yarn around needle clockwise, and knit next st as usual. This operation creates an eyelet hole in the knitting and inc 1 st.

yoke

NOTE: Keep 3 sts at beg and end of each row in garter st throughout body.

Cast on 26 sts.

ROW 1 (RS): k3, place marker, k4, place marker, k12, place marker, k4, place marker, k3.

ROW 2 AND ALL EVEN ROWS: k3, purl to last 3 sts, k3.

ROW 3: Knit.

ROW 5: [Knit to 1 st before marker, KFB, sl marker, KFB] 4 times, knit to end—34 sts.

ROW 7: Knit.

ROW 8: Rep Row 2.

Rep Rows 5–8 2 (3, 4, 5, 6) times more—50 (58, 66, 74, 82) sts.

NEXT ROW (RS): KFB, [knit to 1 st before marker, KFB, sl marker, KFB] 4 times, knit to last st, KFB—60 (68, 76, 84, 92) sts.

NEXT ROW: Rep Row 2.

NEXT ROW (RS): [Knit to marker, sl marker, KFB, knit to 1 st before marker, KFB, sl marker] twice, knit to end—64 (72, 80, 88, 96) sts.

NEXT ROW: Rep Row 2.

Rep the last 4 rows once more—78 (86, 94, 102, 110) sts.

NEXT ROW: Rep Row 5—86 (94, 102, 110, 118) sts.

separate sleeves from body

NEXT ROW (WS): k3, purl to marker, place 20 (22, 24, 26, 28) sts of first sleeve on scrap yarn to be worked later, purl to marker, place 20 (22, 24, 26, 28) sts of second sleeve on scrap yarn to be worked later, purl to last 3 sts, k3—46 (50, 54, 58, 62) sts on needle.

body

ROW 1 (RS): Knit.

ROW 2 AND ALL EVEN ROWS: k3, purl to last 3 sts, k3.

ROW 3: KFB, knit to last st, KFB—48 (52, 56, 60, 64) sts.

ROW 5: Knit.

ROW 7: Rep Row 3—50 (54, 58, 62, 66) sts.

Work in garter st for 5 rows. Bind off.

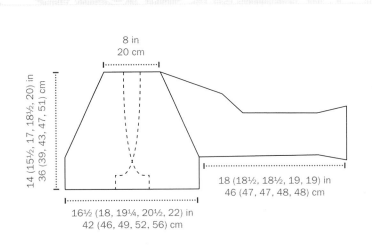

8 in
20 cm

14 (15½, 17, 18½, 20) in
36 (39, 43, 47, 51) cm

18 (18½, 18½, 19, 19) in
46 (47, 47, 48, 48) cm

16½ (18, 19¼, 20½, 22) in
42 (46, 49, 52, 56) cm

sleeves

Transfer 20 (22, 24, 26, 28) held sts of one sleeve to needle. Do not join.

ROW 1 (RS): k10 (11, 12, 13, 14), place marker, knit to end.

ROW 2 AND ALL EVEN ROWS: Purl.

ROW 3: Knit to 2 sts before marker, SSK, sl marker, k2tog, knit to end.

ROW 5: KFB, knit to last st, KFB.

ROW 7: Rep Row 3—18 (20, 22, 24, 26) sts.

Work 21 rows even.

ROW 29: Knit to 1 st before marker, yo, k2, yo, knit to end.

ROW 30: Purl.

ROW 31: Knit.

ROW 32: Purl.

Rep Rows 29–32 twice more—24 (26, 28, 30, 32) sts. Work even until sleeve measures 16½ (17, 17, 17½, 17½)" 42 (43, 43, 44, 44)cm from underarm. Work in garter st for 5 rows. Bind off.

finishing

Seam sleeves. Add a crochet chain loop or oversewn loop buttonhole to left front. Attach button. Weave in ends. Block if desired.

CROPPED CARDIGAN
with leaf ties

With a dramatic scooped neckline and tie front, this three-quarter-length sleeve cardigan is perfect over a lacy blouse or frilly tee. Wear it to fend off the early-morning chill of the first days of fall or spring, or to make that risque translucent top suitable for office wear. The ends of the ties feature sweet leaf details as a finishing touch.

Constructed in typical raglan fashion, the neckline edge is finished with knitted-on i-cord, and the hems with a folded picot edge. The yarn is Cascade Indulgence, a luxurious alpaca/angora blend.

finished measurements
BUST: 32 (34½, 37½, 40, 42½, 45)"
81 (88, 95, 102, 108, 114)cm

yarn
6 (7, 7, 7, 8, 8) balls (123 yards ea) Cascade Yarns Indulgence alpaca/angora blend yarn in color 529 light green

needles
size US 7 (4.5mm) 24" or 29" (61 or 74cm) circular needle

size US 7 (4.5mm) double-pointed needles

If necessary, change needle size to obtain correct gauge.

notions
stitch markers

darning needle

gauge
18 sts and 24 rows = 4" (10cm) in St st

NOTES

[ ] (repeat operation): Rep the bracketed operation the number of times indicated.

sl (slip st[s] or marker): Slip a st or sts purlwise from the left needle to the right needle. Slip a marker from the left needle to the right needle, knitting the sts before and after it as usual.

KFB (knit 1 front and back): Inc 1 st by knitting into the front and back of the next st.

M1 (make 1): Inc 1 st by picking up the bar between the next st and the st just knit and knitting into it.

in patt (in pattern): Cont to work in pattern as est.

work 3 tog (knit or purl 3 together): Dec 2 sts by knitting or purling 3 sts tog as one, in keeping with est patt.

seed st (seed stitch): Knit the purl sts and purl the knit sts.

yo (yarn over): Wrap working yarn around needle clockwise, and knit next st as usual. This operation creates an eyelet hole in the knitting and inc 1 st.

yoke

With circular needle, cast on 64 sts. Do not join.

RAGLAN SET-UP ROW (WS): p1, place marker, p14, place marker, p34, place marker, p14, place marker, p1.

RAGLAN INC ROW (RS): [Knit to 1 st before marker, KFB, sl marker, KFB] 4 times, knit to end—72 sts.

NEXT ROW (WS): Purl.

Rep last 2 rows 18 (21, 24, 27, 30, 33) times more—216 (240, 264, 288, 312, 336) sts.

separate sleeves from body

NEXT ROW (RS): Knit to marker, place next 52 (58, 64, 70, 76, 82) sts for first sleeve on scrap yarn to be worked later, knit to marker, place next 52 (58, 64, 70, 76, 82) sts for second sleeve on scrap yarn to be worked later, knit to end—112 (124, 136, 148, 160, 172) sts on needle.

body

Work 15 rows even.

NEXT ROW (RS): KFB, knit to last st, KFB—114 (126, 138, 150, 162, 174) sts.

NEXT ROW (WS): KFB, purl to last st, KFB—116 (128, 140, 152, 164, 176) sts.

Rep last 2 rows twice more, then work RS row only once more—128 (140, 152, 164, 176, 188) sts.

Cont in St st, cast on 9 sts at beg of next 2 rows—146 (158, 170, 182, 194, 200) sts. Work even until body measures

10" (25cm) from underarm, ending with a WS row.

EYELET ROW (RS): k2, [yo, k2tog] to end.

Work even in St st for 1½" (4cm) more. Bind off.

sleeves

Transfer 52 (58, 64, 70, 76, 82) held sts of one sleeve to needle. Do not join. Work even in St st until sleeve measures 9½ (10, 10, 10, 10½, 10½)" 24 (25, 25, 25, 27, 27)cm from underarm, ending with a WS row.

EYELET ROW (RS): k2, [yo, k2tog] to end.

Work even in St st for 1½" (4cm) more. Bind off.

finishing

Seam sleeves. Fold sleeve and body hems to WS on eyelet row. With yarn threaded on a darning needle, slip sts in place.

ties and neck edging

LEAF

With DPNs, cast on 1 st. Working in seed st, inc 1 st at beg of next 14 rows—15 sts.

NEXT ROW: Work 6 sts in patt, work 3 tog, work to end—13 sts.

NEXT ROW: Work even in seed st.

NEXT ROW: Work 2 sts in patt, work 3 tog, work 3 sts in patt, work 3 tog, work to end—9 sts.

NEXT ROW: Work even in seed st.

Cont in seed st, dec 1 st at beg of next 4 rows—5 sts.

I-CORD

Work i-cord on these 5 sts as foll: Knit 1 row, do not turn. *Slide sts back to working end of needle and knit them again. Rep from * for 11" (28cm). Do not bind off.

Now work applied i-cord around neckline as foll: *k4 on DPN, then knit last st tog with 1 st picked up from right front neck edge—5 sts. Slide sts back to working end of needle and rep from *. Work as est all around neckline, then cont working i-cord for 11" (28cm) more.

END WITH LEAF WORKED IN REVERSE

Work in seed st, inc 1 st at beg of next 4 rows—9 sts.

NEXT ROW: Work even in seed st.

NEXT ROW: Work 2 sts in patt, M1, work 1, M1, work 3 sts in patt, M1, k1, M1, work to end—13 sts.

NEXT ROW: Work even in seed st.

NEXT ROW: Work 6 sts in pattern, M1, k1, M1, work to end—15 sts.

Cont in seed st, dec 1 st at beg of next 14 rows—1 st.

Fasten off. Weave in ends. Block if desired.

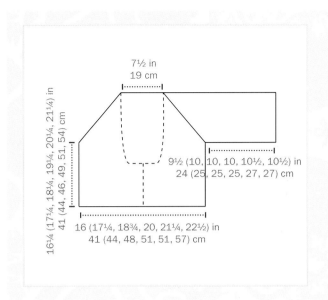

7½ in
19 cm

16¼ (17¼, 18¼, 19¼, 20¼, 21¼) in
41 (44, 46, 49, 51, 54) cm

9½ (10, 10, 10, 10½, 10½) in
24 (25, 25, 25, 27, 27) cm

16 (17¼, 18¾, 20, 21¼, 22½) in
41 (44, 48, 51, 51, 57) cm

AIRY WRAP-AROUND
lace sweater

Made with gossamer-soft mohair worked on big needles, this light-weight wrap sweater has an open, airy feel. It's the perfect thing to wear when your expectations for it to be spring already don't match up with the reality of snow in March. Layer it on over a tank top and you'll at least look like spring, even if the trees stubbornly refuse to bud and the ground stubbornly refuses to thaw.

Because of the nature of the wrap sweater, one size fits many body shapes. The back is tapered, so the sweater hangs close to the body, even if worn open.

finished measurements
BUST: 33½ (37, 40, 43, 46½)"
85 (94, 102, 109, 118)cm

yarn
5 (5, 6, 6, 7) balls (165 yards ea)
Plymouth Yarns/Lane Cervinia Softer
mohair/nylon blend yarn in color
3131 lilac

needles
size US 11 (8mm) circular needle in
any length

*If necessary, change needle size to
obtain correct gauge.*

notions
removable stitch markers or safety pins

darning needle

gauge
10 sts and 16 rows = 4" (10cm) in
St st

NOTES

[ ] (repeat operation): Rep the bracketed operation the number of times indicated.

sl (slip st[s] or marker): Slip a st or sts purlwise from the left needle to the right needle. Slip a marker from the left needle to the right needle, knitting the sts before and after it as usual.

SSK (slip, slip, knit): Dec 1 st by slipping 2 sts knitwise one at a time, inserting tip of left needle into both sts and knitting the 2 sts tog.

k2tog (knit 2 together): Dec 1 st by knitting 2 sts tog.

yo (yarn over): Wrap working yarn around needle clockwise, and knit next st as usual. This operation creates an eyelet hole in the knitting and inc 1 st.

in patt (in pattern): Cont to work in pattern as est.

yoke

Cast on 34 sts. Do not join.

ROW 1 (WS): p1, place marker in next st, purl this st, p5, place marker in next st, purl this st, p18, place marker in next st, purl this st, p5, place marker in next st, purl this st, p1.

ROW 2: k1, yo, knit marked st, yo, k5, yo, knit marked st, yo, k18, yo, knit marked st, yo, k5, yo, knit marked st, yo, k1.

ROW 3: Purl.

ROW 4: [Knit to marked st, yo, knit marked st, yo] 4 times, knit to end.

Rep Rows 3–4 10 (12, 14, 16, 18) times more—130 (146, 162, 178, 194) sts.

separate sleeves from body

NEXT ROW (WS): p13 (15, 17, 19, 21) front sts, place next 31 (35, 39, 43, 47) sts for first sleeve on scrap yarn to be worked later, p42 (46, 50, 54, 58) back sts, place next 31 (35, 39, 43, 47) sts for second sleeve on scrap yarn to be worked later, p13 (15, 17, 19, 21) front sts—68 (76, 84, 92, 100) sts on needle.

Place a marker at center back, 34 (38, 42, 46, 50) sts in from each edge of body.

body

Work 2 rows even.

DEC ROW (RS): Knit to 2 sts before center back marker, SSK, sl marker, k2tog, knit to end.

Work 3 rows even. Rep last 4 rows twice more—62 (70, 78, 86, 94) sts. Work 16 rows even, ending with a WS row.

cable border

Purl 1 row, knit 1 row, purl 2 rows.

CABLE SET-UP ROW (RS): p3 (3, 4, 3, 2), [work chart A over next 6 sts, p1 (2, 1, 2, 3)] 4 (4, 5, 5, 5) times, [work chart B over next 6 sts, p1 (2, 1, 2, 3)] 4 (4, 5, 5, 5) times, p3 (3, 4, 3, 2).

NEXT ROW (WS): Work all sts as they appear (knit the knits and purl the purls).

Cont in patt as est for 16 more rows. Purl 1 row, knit 1 row, purl 1 row. Bind off loosely.

sleeves

Transfer 31 (35, 39, 43, 47) held sts of one sleeve to needle. Work even in St st for 10 (10, 11, 11, 11)" 25 (25, 28, 28, 28)cm, ending with a WS row.

cable border

Purl 1 row, knit 1 row, purl 2 rows.

CABLE SET-UP ROW (RS): p1 (1, 1, 3, 2), [work cable chart A over next 6 sts, p1 (2, 3, 3, 1)] 2 (2, 2, 2, 3) times, [work cable chart B over next 6 sts, p1 (2, 3, 3, 1)] 2 (2, 2, 2, 3) times, p2 (2, 2, 4, 3).

NEXT ROW (WS): Work all sts as they appear.

Cont in patt as est for 16 more rows. Purl 1 row, knit 1 row, purl 1 row. Bind off loosely.

front

With RS facing, pick up and knit 39 sts along right front edge.

ROWS 1–7: Work in St st.

ROW 8 (RS): k3, [yo, k2tog, k6] 4 times, yo, k2tog, k2.

ROW 9: Purl.

ROW 10: k1, [k2tog, yo, k1, yo, k2tog, k3] 4 times, k2tog, yo, k1, yo, k2tog, k1.

ROW 11: Purl.

ROW 12: Rep Row 7.

Rep Rows 1–12 for 45 (45, 50, 50, 55)" 114 (114, 127, 127, 140)cm.

eyelet border

ROWS 1–10: Work in garter st, dec 1 st at beg of each row—29 sts.

ROW 11: k1, [yo, k2tog] to end.

ROWS 12–15: Work in garter st, dec 2 st at beg of each row—25 sts.

Rep Rows 11–15 once more—21 sts. Bind off. Work left front same as right.

finishing

Seam sleeves. Weave in ends.

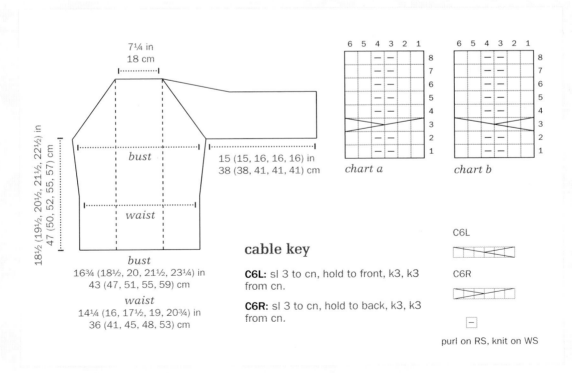

7¼ in
18 cm

18½ (19½, 20½, 21½, 22½) in
47 (50, 52, 55, 57) cm

bust

waist

15 (15, 16, 16, 16) in
38 (38, 41, 41, 41) cm

bust
16¾ (18½, 20, 21½, 23¼) in
43 (47, 51, 55, 59) cm

waist
14¼ (16, 17½, 19, 20¾) in
36 (41, 45, 48, 53) cm

chart a

chart b

cable key

C6L: sl 3 to cn, hold to front, k3, k3 from cn.

C6R: sl 3 to cn, hold to back, k3, k3 from cn.

C6L

C6R

purl on RS, knit on WS

PUFF-SLEEVED
feminine cardigan

This puff-sleeved sweater is inspired by the strong and feminine heroines of Victorian-era novels and by the tough and beautiful stars of television shows detailing American frontier life, as well as by modern fashion. I love history and costume, and I really enjoy creating clothing that brings out the beauty and femininity of the wearer. This sweater is incredibly feminine and curvy, with little details that draw attention to the collar, bust and waist.

From the mandarin collar to the delicately puffed sleeves, shaping at waist and bust, and highly decorated peplum, this sweater is all girl. Knit from Knit Picks Merino Style in the color Maple Leaf, the cardigan's bright red color amps up the soft, feminine styling.

finished measurements
BUST: 34 (36, 38, 40, 42)"
86 (91, 97, 102, 107)cm

yarn
5 (6, 6, 7, 7) skeins (123 yards ea) Knit Picks Merino Style 100% wool yarn in color 461 Maple Leaf

needles
size US 6 (4mm) 29" (74cm) circular needle

size US 4 (3.5mm) circular or straight needles

If necessary, change needle size to obtain correct gauge.

notions
stitch markers

stitch holders or scrap yarn

sewing needle and thread

darning needle

8 (8, 8, 9, 9) ½" (1cm) buttons

gauge
22 sts and 30 rows = 4" (10cm) in St st on larger needles

NOTES

[ ] (repeat operation): Rep the bracketed operation the number of times indicated.

sl (slip st[s] or marker): Slip a st or sts purlwise from the left needle to the right needle. Slip a marker from the left needle to the right needle, knitting the sts before and after it as usual.

KFB (knit 1 front and back): Inc 1 st by knitting into the front and back of the next st.

SSK (slip, slip, knit): Dec 1 st by slipping 2 sts knitwise one at a time, inserting tip of left needle into both sts and knitting the 2 sts tog.

M1 (make 1): Inc 1 st by picking up the bar between the next st and the st just knit and knitting into it.

work 2 tog (knit or purl 2 together): Dec 1 st by knitting or purling 2 sts tog as one, in keeping with est patt.

k2tog (knit 2 together): Dec 1 st by knitting 2 sts tog.

seed st (seed stitch): Knit the purl sts and purl the knit sts.

collar

With larger needle, cast on 62 (66, 70, 74, 78, 82, 86) sts. Do not join.

ROWS 1–10: KFB in first st, work in seed st to end—72 (76, 80, 84, 88, 92, 96) sts.

ROWS 11–17: Work even in seed st.

ROW 18 (WS): Purl.

Purl 1 row, knit 1 row, purl 2 more rows.

yoke

ROW 1 (RS): k12 (13, 14, 15, 16), KFB, place marker, KFB, k8, KFB, place marker, KFB, k24 (26, 28, 30, 32), KFB, place marker, KFB, k8, KFB, place marker, KFB, k12 (13, 14, 15, 16)—80 (84, 88, 92, 96) sts.

ROW 2 (WS): Purl.

ROW 3: [Knit to 1 st before marker, KFB, sl marker, KFB] 4 times, knit to end—88 (92, 96, 100, 104) sts.

ROW 4: Purl.

Rep Rows 3–4 5 times more—128 (132, 136, 140, 144) sts.

NEXT ROW (RS) (SLEEVE POUF INCREASES): *Knit to 1 st before marker, KFB, sl marker, KFB, k1, [M1, k3] 7 times, KFB, sl marker, KFB; rep from * once more, knit to end—150 (154, 158, 162, 166) sts.

Purl 1 row. Rep Rows 3–4 25 (27, 29, 31, 33) times more—350 (370, 390, 410, 430) sts.

separate sleeves from body

NEXT ROW: Knit front sts, place next 83 (87, 91, 95, 99) sts for first sleeve on scrap yarn to be worked later, knit back sts, place next 83 (87, 91, 95, 99) sts for second sleeve on scrap yarn to be worked later, knit to end—184 (196, 208, 220, 232) sts on needle.

body

Work even in St st for 17 rows.

WAIST SHAPING SET-UP ROW (RS): k24 (27, 28, 31, 32), place marker, k44 (44, 48, 48, 52), place marker, k48 (54, 56, 62, 64), place marker, k44 (44, 48, 48, 52), place marker, knit to end.

Purl 1 row.

waist shaping

ROW 1 (RS): Knit to 2 sts before front marker, SSK, sl marker, k1, k2tog, knit to 3 sts before first back marker, SSK, k1, sl marker, k2tog, knit to 2 sts before second back marker, SSK, sl marker, k1, k2tog, knit to 3 sts before second front marker, SSK, k1, sl marker, k2tog, knit to end—176 (188, 200, 212, 224) sts.

ROW 2 AND ALL EVEN ROWS (WS): Purl.

ROW 3: Knit.

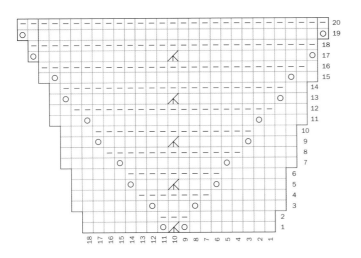

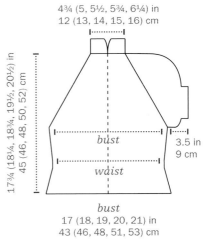

4¾ (5, 5½, 5¾, 6¼) in
12 (13, 14, 15, 16) cm

17¾ (18¼, 18¾, 19½, 20½) in
45 (46, 48, 50, 52) cm

bust

waist

3.5 in
9 cm

bust
17 (18, 19, 20, 21) in
43 (46, 48, 51, 53) cm

waist
14½ (15½, 16¾, 17¾, 19) in
37 (39, 43, 45, 48) cm

dashed lines indicate purl on RS, knit on WS; yarn over is indicated by circles; and k3tog is indicated by diagonal lines with carets.

ROW 5: Knit to 2 sts before front marker, SSK, sl marker, k1, k2tog, knit to 3 sts before second front marker, SSK, k1, sl marker, k2tog, knit to end—172 (184, 196, 208, 220) sts.

ROW 7: Knit.

ROW 9: Rep Row 1—164 (176, 188, 200, 212) sts.

ROW 11: Knit.

ROW 13: Rep Row 5—160 (172, 184, 196, 208) sts.

Work 7 rows even, ending with a WS row.

peplum

Purl 1 row, knit 1 row, purl 2 rows, knit 2 rows, purl 1 row, knit 1 row.

NEXT ROW (RS) (LACE SET-UP ROW): k7, work 3 (3, 4, 4, 4) repeats of chart pattern beg at Row 1, k37 (49, 25, 37, 49), work 3 (3, 4, 4, 4) repeats of chart pattern beg at Row 1, k8.

Cont as est to end of chart, ending with a WS row. Knit 2 rows, purl 1 row, knit 2 rows, purl 2 rows, knit 1 row, purl 1 row. Bind off loosely.

sleeves

Transfer the 83 (87, 91, 95, 99) held sts of one sleeve to the larger needle. Do not join. Beg with a purl row (WS), work even for 11 rows.

ROW 12 (RS): k5 (7, 4, 6, 4), SSK, [k7, SSK] 8 (8, 9, 9, 10) times, k4 (6, 4, 6, 3)—74 (78, 81, 85, 88) sts.

ROWS 13 AND 15: Purl.

ROW 14: k4 (6, 3, 5, 3), SSK, [k6, SSK] 8 (8, 9, 9, 10) times, knit to end—65 (69, 71, 75, 77) sts.

ROW 16: k3 (5, 2, 4, 2), SSK, [k5, SSK] 8 (8, 9, 9, 10) times, knit to end—56 (60, 61, 65, 66) sts.

ROW 17: Purl.

ROW 18: k2 (4, 1, 3, 1), SSK, [k4, SSK] 8 (8, 9, 9, 10) times, knit to end—47 (51, 51, 55, 55) sts.

Purl 2 rows, knit 1 row, purl 2 rows, knit 2 rows, purl 1 row, knit 2 rows, purl 2 rows, knit 1 row, purl 1 row. Bind off loosely.

finishing

button band

With RS facing and using smaller needles, pick up and knit 3 sts for every 4 rows along left front edge. Work 7 rows in seed st. Bind off.

buttonhole band

With RS facing and using smaller needles, pick up and knit 3 sts for every 4 rows along right front edge. Place 8 (8, 8, 9, 9) markers for buttonholes, evenly spaced along edge. Work 3 rows in seed st.

NEXT ROW: Work in seed st to marker, [yo, work 2 tog, work in seed st to marker] 7 (7, 7, 8, 8) times, yo, work 2 tog, work in seed st to end.

Work 3 more rows seed st. Bind off.

Seam sleeves. Weave in ends. Attach buttons. Block if desired.

SHORT-SLEEVED CARDIGAN
with ribbing

This sweater combines the ease of bulky yarn (Cascade Bulky) with subtle details like shaping at the back and sleeves for a look that is casual and crisp at the same time. The deep bordered ribbing provides a structured frame for this easygoing knit. Choose a bright color and wear it to usher in the warmer months.

This sweater is knit from neckline to hem using both decreases and change in needle and stitch pattern to create shaping at the back and in the sleeves. The button band is picked up and knit at the very end.

finished measurements
BUST: 34 (36, 38, 40, 42)"
86 (91, 97, 102, 107)cm

yarn
5 (5, 5, 6, 6) skeins (128 yards ea)
Cascade 128 wool yarn in color 6240
yellow

needles
size US 10 (6mm) 29" (74cm) circular
needle

size US 8 (5mm) 29" (74cm) circular
needle

size US 10 (6mm) double-pointed
needles

size US 8 (5mm) double-pointed
needles

*If necessary, change needle size to
obtain correct gauge.*

notions
stitch holders or scrap yarn

removable markers or safety pins

darning needle

seven 1" (3cm) buttons

sewing needle and thread

gauge
14 sts and 20 rows = 4" (10cm) in St
st on larger needles

NOTES

[ ] (repeat operation): Rep the bracketed operation the number of times indicated.

sl (slip st[s] or marker): Slip a st or sts purlwise from the left needle to the right needle. Slip a marker from the left needle to the right needle, knitting the sts before and after it as usual.

k2tog (knit 2 together): Dec 1 st by knitting 2 sts tog.

p2tog (purl 2 together): Dec 1 st by purling 2 sts tog.

SSK (slip, slip, knit): Dec 1 st by slipping 2 sts knitwise one at a time, inserting tip of left needle into both sts and knitting the 2 sts tog.

yo (yarn over): Wrap working yarn around needle clockwise, and knit next st as usual. This operation creates an eyelet hole in the knitting and inc 1 st.

yoke

With smaller circular needle, cast on 67 (71, 75, 81, 83) sts. Purl 1 row, knit 2 rows, purl 2 rows, knit 1 row, then purl 2 more rows. Change to larger needle.

RAGLAN SET-UP ROW (RS): k14 (15, 16, 16, 17), place marker, k5 (5, 5, 7, 7), place marker, k28 (30, 32, 34, 34), place marker, k5 (5, 5, 7, 7), place marker, k15 (16, 17, 17, 18).

NEXT ROW AND ALL WS ROWS: Purl.

RAGLAN INC ROW (RS): [Knit to marker, yo, sl marker, k1, yo] 4 times, knit to end—75 (79, 83, 89, 91) sts.

Work raglan incs as est on every RS row 14 (15, 16, 17, 18) times more—187 (199, 211, 225, 235) sts.

separate sleeves from body

NEXT ROW (WS): p29 (31, 33, 34, 36) front sts, place marker for right side, place next 36 (38, 40, 44, 46) sleeve sts on scrap yarn, p57 (61, 65, 69, 71) back sts, place next 36 (38, 40, 44, 46) sleeve sts on scrap yarn, place marker for left side, p29 (31, 33, 34, 36) front sts—115 (123, 131, 137, 143) sts on needle.

body

Work 13 (13, 15, 15, 17) rows even.

center back decreases

ROW 1 (WS): Purl front sts, p28 (30, 32, 34, 35), place a removable marker in the next (center back) st, purl to end.

ROW 2: Knit to 2 sts before center back st, SSK, k1, k2tog—113 (121, 129, 135, 141) sts.

ROW 3 AND ALL WS ROWS: Purl.

ROW 4: Knit.

ROW 6: Rep Row 2—111 (119, 127, 133, 139) sts.

ROW 8: Knit.

ROW 9: Rep Row 2—109 (117, 125, 131, 137) sts.

ROW 10: Purl.

bordered ribbing

Change to smaller needle and purl 1 row. Knit 1 row, purl 2 rows, knit 2 rows, purl 1 row.

NEXT ROW: Knit, inc 0 (0, 0, 2, 0) sts evenly spaced—109 (117, 125, 133, 137) sts.

RIBBING SET-UP ROW (RS): k3, [p2, k2] to last 6 sts, p2, k2, k2tog—108 (116, 124, 132, 136) sts.

NEXT ROW (WS): p3, [k2, p2] to last 5 sts, k2, p3.

NEXT ROW (RS): k3, [p2, k2] to last 5 sts, p2, k3.

Rep last 2 rows 17 times more, then work WS row once more. Knit 1 row, purl 1 row, knit 2 rows, purl 2 rows, knit 1 row, purl 1 row. Bind off loosely.

sleeves

Transfer 36 (38, 40, 44, 46) held sts of one sleeve to larger DPNs.

RND 1: Pick up and knit 2 sts at underarm to close the hole produced when joining the fronts to the back, knit to end—38 (40, 42, 46, 48) sts.

RND 2 AND ALL EVEN RNDS: Knit.

RND 3: k19 (20, 21, 23, 24), place marker, k19 (20, 21, 23, 24).

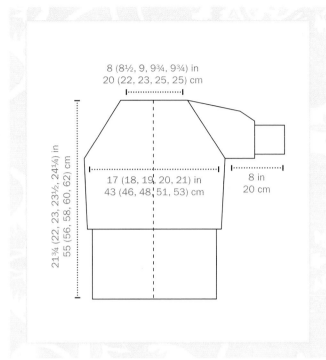

8 (8½, 9, 9¾, 9¾) in
20 (22, 23, 25, 25) cm

21¾ (22, 23, 23½, 24¼) in
55 (56, 58, 60, 62) cm

17 (18, 19, 20, 21) in
43 (46, 48, 51, 53) cm

8 in
20 cm

RND 5: Knit.

RND 7: Knit to 2 sts before marker, SSK, sl marker, k2tog, knit to end—36 (38, 40, 44, 46) sts.

RND 9: Knit.

RND 11: Rep Rnd 7—34 (36, 38, 42, 44) sts.

Knit 2 rnds even.

bordered ribbing

Change to smaller DPNs. Purl 3 rnds, knit 2 rnds, purl 3 rnds.

NEXT RND: Knit, dec 0 (2, 0, 0, 2) sts evenly spaced—36 (36, 40, 44, 44) sts.

Work in k2, p2 rib for 15 rnds. Knit 1 rnd, purl 3 rnds, knit 2 rnds, purl 3 rnds. Bind off loosely.

finishing

buttonhole band

With RS facing and beg at hemline edge, using smaller circular needle, pick up and knit 66 (66, 68, 70, 70) sts along the right front. Purl 2 rows, knit 1 row.

NEXT ROW (RS): p2 (2, 3, 4, 4), yo, p2tog, (p8, yo, p2tog) 6 times, p2 (2, 3, 4, 4).

Purl 1 row, knit 2 rows, purl 1 row, knit 1 more row. Bind off.

button band

With RS facing and beg at neckline edge, using smaller circular needle, pick up and knit 66 (66, 68, 70, 70) sts along the left front. Purl 2 rows, knit 1 row, purl 2 rows, knit 2 rows, purl 1 row, knit 1 more row. Bind off all sts.

Attach buttons. Weave in ends. Block if desired.

ELIZABETH BENNET
cabled cardigan

"It is a truth universally acknowledged, that a single man in possession of a good fortune, must be in want of a wife." So Jane Austen begins her much-loved Georgian novel, *Pride and Prejudice*. Who knows, if Elizabeth Bennet had been wearing this romantic cardigan, she and Mr. Darcy might have settled their misunderstandings more quickly.

Cabling details and puffy sleeves give this simple raglan cardigan a soft retro feel. The plush halo of the wool/angora yarn adds to the feminine styling. This cardigan is shaped using the same basic principles as the Puff-Sleeved Cardigan (page 66), only with longer, flared and cabled sleeves and a fitted cabled bodice. Wear this sweet sweater when you're ready to capture your own Mr. Darcy.

finished measurements
BUST: 34 (36, 38, 40, 42, 44, 46)"
86 (91, 97, 102, 107, 112, 117)cm

yarn
17 (18, 19, 20, 21, 22, 24) balls (109 yards ea) Cascade Yarns Cloud 9 wool/angora blend yarn in color 114 lavender.

needles
size US 6 (4mm) 29" (74cm) circular needle

size US 4 (3.5mm) circular or straight needles

If necessary, change needle size to obtain correct gauge.

notions
stitch markers

stitch holders or scrap yarn

darning needle

9 (9, 10, 10, 11, 11, 12) ½" (3cm) buttons

sewing needle and thread

gauge
22 sts and 30 rows = 4" (10cm) in St st on larger needles

NOTES

[ ] (repeat operation): Rep the bracketed operation the number of times indicated.

sl (slip st[s] or marker): Slip a st or sts purlwise from the left needle to the right needle. Slip a marker from the left needle to the right needle, knitting the sts before and after it as usual.

work 2 tog (knit or purl 2 together): Dec 1 st by knitting or purling 2 sts tog as one, in keeping with est patt.

k2tog (knit 2 together): Dec 1 st by knitting 2 sts tog.

KFB (knit 1 front and back): Inc 1 st by knitting into the front and back of the next st.

SSK (slip, slip, knit): Dec 1 st by slipping 2 sts knitwise one at a time, inserting tip of left needle into both sts and knitting the 2 sts tog.

M1 (make 1): Inc 1 st by picking up the bar between the next st and the st just knit and knitting into it.

seed st (seed stitch): Knit the purl sts and purl the knit sts.

collar

With larger needle, cast on 62 (66, 70, 74, 78, 82, 86) sts. Do not join.

ROWS 1–10: KFB in first st, work in seed st to end—72 (76, 80, 84, 88, 92, 96) sts.

ROWS 11–17: Work even in seed st.

Beg with a WS row, purl 2 rows, knit 1 row, then purl 2 more rows.

yoke

ROW 1 (RS): k12 (13, 14, 15, 16, 17, 18), KFB, place marker, KFB, k8, KFB, place marker, KFB, k24 (26, 28, 30, 32, 34, 36), KFB, place marker, KFB, k8, KFB, place marker, KFB, k12 (13, 14, 15, 16, 17, 18)—80 (84, 88, 92, 96, 100, 104) sts.

ROW 2 (WS): Purl.

ROW 3: [Knit to 1 st before marker, KFB, sl marker, KFB] 4 times, knit to end—88 (92, 96, 100, 104, 108, 112) sts.

ROW 4: Purl.

Rep Rows 3–4 5 times more—128 (132, 136, 140, 144, 148, 152) sts.

NEXT ROW (RS) (SLEEVE POUF INC): *Knit to 1 st before marker, KFB, sl marker, KFB, k1, [m1, k3] 7 times, KFB, sl marker, KFB; rep from * once more, knit to end—150 (154, 158, 162, 166, 170, 174) sts.

Purl 1 row. Rep Rows 3–4 25 (27, 29, 31, 33, 35, 37) times more—350 (370, 390, 410, 430, 450, 470) sts.

separate sleeves from body

NEXT ROW: Knit front sts, place next 83 (87, 91, 95, 99, 103, 107) sts for first sleeve on scrap yarn to be worked later, knit back sts, place next 83 (87, 91, 95, 99, 103, 107) sts for second sleeve on scrap yarn to be worked later, knit to end—184 (196, 208, 220, 232, 244, 256) sts on needle.

body

Work even in St st for 17 rows.

NEXT ROW (RS) (WAIST-SHAPING SET-UP ROW): k24 (27, 28, 31, 32, 36, 37), place marker, k44 (44, 48, 48, 52, 52, 56), place marker, k48 (54, 56, 62, 64, 68, 70), place marker, k44 (44, 48, 48, 52, 52, 56), place marker, knit to end.

Purl 1 row.

waist shaping

ROW 1 (RS): Knit to 2 sts before front marker, SSK, sl marker, k1, k2tog, knit to 3 sts before first back marker, SSK, k1, sl marker, k2tog, knit to 2 sts before second back marker, SSK, sl marker, k1, k2tog, knit to 3 sts before second front marker, SSK, k1, sl marker, k2tog, knit to end—176 (188, 200, 212, 224, 236, 248) sts.

ROW 2 AND ALL WS ROWS: Purl.

ROW 3: Knit.

ROW 5: Knit to 2 sts before front marker, SSK, sl marker, k1, k2tog, knit to 3 sts before second front marker, SSK, k1, sl marker, k2tog, knit to end—172 (184, 196, 208, 220, 232, 244) sts.

cable key

C6L: sl 3 to cn, hold to front, k3, k3 from cn.

C6R: sl 3 to cn, hold to back, k3, k3 from cn.

T3L: sl 2 to cn, hold to front, p1, k2 from cn.

T3R: sl 1 to cn, hold to back, k2, p1 from cn.

IC6L (inc cable 6 left): sl 3 to cn and hold in front. k2, KFB, k3 from cn.

IC6R (inc cable 6 right): sl 3 to cn and hold in back. k2, KFB, k3 from cn.

C7L: sl 4 to cn and hold in front. k3, [p1, k3] from cn.

C7R: sl 4 to cn and hold in back. k3, [p1, k3] from cn.

IC7L (inc cable 7 left): sl 4 to cn and hold in front. k2, KFB, [p1, k3] from cn.

IC7R (inc cable 7 right): sl 4 to CN and hold in back. k2, KFB, [p1, k3] from cn.

C8L: sl 5 to cn and hold in front. k3, [p2, k3] from cn.

C8R: sl 5 to CN and hold in back. k3, [p2, k3] from cn.

T4L: sl 3 to CN, hold to front, p1, k3 from cn.

T4R: sl 1 to CN, hold to back, k3, p1 from cn.

DC8L (dec cable 8 left): sl 4 to cn and hold in front. k2, k2tog, k4 from cn.

DC8R (dec cable 8 right): sl 4 to cn and hold in back. k4, [k2tog, k2] from cn.

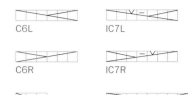
C6L   IC7L

C6R   IC7R

T3L   C8L

T3R   C8R

IC6L   T4L

IC6R   T4R

C7L   DC8L

C7R   DC8R

■
no stitch

□ −
purl on RS, knit on WS

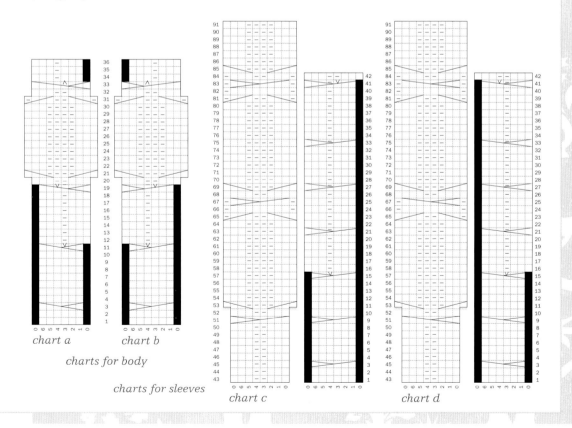

chart a   *chart b*

charts for body

charts for sleeves

chart c   *chart d*

ROW 7: Knit.

ROW 9: Rep Row 1—164 (176, 188, 200, 212, 224, 236) sts.

ROW 11: Knit.

ROW 13: Rep Row 5—160 (172, 184, 196, 208, 220, 232) sts.

Work 7 rows even, inc 0 (3, 6, 2, 0, 1, 0) st(s) evenly across last WS row—160 (175, 190, 198, 208, 221, 232) sts.

cabled waist

Beg with a RS row, purl 1 row. Knit 1 row, purl 2 rows, knit 2 rows, purl 1 row, knit 2 rows, purl 1 more row.

{ SIZE 34 }
ROW 1 (RS CABLE SET-UP ROW): p2, [k6, p4] 15 times, k6, p2.

ROW 2: k2, p6, [k4, p6] 15 times, k2.

ROW 3: p2, [work row 3 of chart A, p4] 4 times, [work row 3 of chart B, p4] 4 times, [work row 3 of chart A, p4] 4 times, [work row 3 of chart B, p4] 3 times, work row 3 of chart B, p2.

{ SIZE 36 }
ROW 1 (RS CABLE SET-UP ROW): p2 [k6, p5] 15 times, k6, p2.

ROW 2: k2, p6, [k5, p6] 15 times, k2.

ROW 3: p2, [work row 3 of chart A, p5] 4 times, [work row 3 of chart B, p5] 4 times, [work row 3 of chart A, p5] 4 times, [work row 3 of chart B, p5] 3 times, work row 3 of chart B, p2.

{ SIZE 38 }
ROW 1 (RS CABLE SET-UP ROW): p2, [k6, p6] 15 times, k6, p2.

ROW 2: k2, p6, [k6, p6] 15 times, k2.

ROW 3: p2, [work row 3 of chart A, p6] 4 times, [work row 3 of chart B, p6] 4 times, [work row 3 of chart A, p6] 4 times, [work row 3 of chart B, p6] 3 times, work row 3 of chart B, p2.

{ SIZE 40 }
ROW 1 (RS CABLE SET-UP ROW): p2, [k6, p4] 19 times, k6, p2.

ROW 2: k2, p6, [k4, p6] 19 times, k2.

ROW 3: p2, [work row 3 of chart A, p4] 5 times, [work row 3 of chart B, p4] 5 times, [work row 3 of chart A, p4] 5 times, [work row 3 of chart B, p4] 4 times, work row 3 of chart B, p2.

{ SIZE 42 }
ROW 1 (RS CABLE SET-UP ROW): p3, [k6, p4] 5 times, p2, [k6, p4] 5 times, p2, [k6, p4] 5 times, p2, [k6, p4] 4 times, k6, p3.

ROW 2: k3, p6, [k4, p6] 4 times, k2, [k4, p6] 5 times, k2, [k4, p6] 5 times, k2, [k4, p6] 5 times, k3.

ROW 3: p3, [work row 3 of chart A, p4] 5 times, p2, [work row 3 of chart B, p4] 5 times, p2, [work row 3 of chart A, p4] 5 times, p2, [work row 3 of chart B, p4] 4 times, work row 3 of chart B, p3.

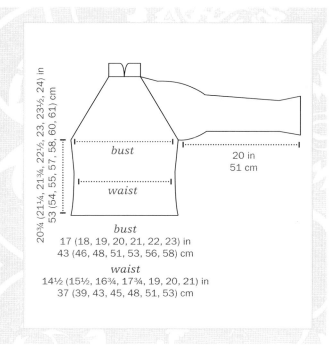

20¾ (21¼, 21¾, 22¼, 23, 23½, 24) in
53 (54, 55, 57, 58, 60, 61) cm

bust

waist

20 in
51 cm

bust
17 (18, 19, 20, 21, 22, 23) in
43 (46, 48, 51, 53, 56, 58) cm

waist
14½ (15½, 16¾, 17¾, 19, 20, 21) in
37 (39, 43, 45, 48, 51, 53) cm

{ SIZE 44 }

ROW 1 (RS CABLE SET-UP ROW): p3, [k6, p5] 19 times, k6, p3.

ROW 2: k3, p6, [k5, p6] 19 times, k3.

ROW 3: p3, [work row 3 of chart A, p5] 5 times, [work row 3 of chart B, p5] 5 times, [work row 3 of chart A, p5] 5 times, [work row 3 of chart B, p5] 4 times, work row 3 of chart B, p3.

{ SIZE 46 }

ROW 1 (RS CABLE SET-UP ROW): p4, [k6, p5] 5 times, p3, [k6, p5] 5 times, p3, [k6, p5] 5 times, p3, [k6, p5] 4 times, k6, p4.

ROW 2: k4, p6, [k5, p6] 4 times, k3, [k5, p6] 5 times, k3, [k5, p6] 5 times, k3, [k5, p6] 5 times, k4.

ROW 3: p4, [work row 3 of chart A, p5] 5 times, p3, [work row 3 of chart B, p5] 5 times, p3, [work row 3 of chart A, p5] 5 times, p3, [work row 3 of chart B, p5] 4 times, work row 3 of chart B, p4.

{ ALL SIZES }

Cont as est to end of cable charts, ending with a WS row. Knit 2 rows, purl 1 row, knit 2 rows, purl 2 rows, knit 1 row, then purl 1 row. Bind off loosely.

finishing
button band

With RS facing, using smaller needles, pick up and knit 3 sts for every 4 rows along left front edge. Work 7 rows in seed st. Bind off.

buttonhole band

With RS facing, using smaller needles, pick up and knit 3 sts for every 4 rows along right front edge. Place 9 (9, 10, 10, 11, 11, 12) markers for buttonholes, evenly spaced. Work 2 rows seed st.

NEXT ROW: Work in seed st to marker, [yo, work 2 tog, work to next marker] 8 (8, 9, 9, 10, 10, 11) times, yo, k2tog, work to end.

Work 4 more rows in seed st. Bind off.

sleeves

Transfer the 83 (87, 91, 95, 99, 103, 107) held sts of one sleeve to the larger needle. Do not join. Beg with a WS row, work even for 11 rows.

ROW 12 (RS): k5 (7, 4, 6, 4, 6, 8), SSK, [k7, ssk] 8 (8, 9, 9, 10, 10, 10) times, k4 (6, 4, 6, 3, 5, 7)—74 (78, 81, 85, 88, 92, 96) sts.

ROW 13 AND ALL WS ROWS THROUGH ROW 17: Purl.

ROW 14: k4 (6, 3, 5, 3, 5, 7), SSK, [k6, SSK] 8 (8, 9, 9, 10, 10, 10) times, knit to end—65 (69, 71, 75, 77, 81, 85) sts.

ROW 16: k3 (5, 2, 4, 2, 4, 6), SSK, [k5, SSK] 8 (8, 9, 9, 10, 10, 10) times, knit to end—56 (60, 61, 65, 66, 70, 74) sts.

ROW 18: Knit.

ROW 19: Purl, adjusting st counts as foll: inc 4 (0, 0, 0, 0) sts evenly spaced; dec 0 (0, 1, 0, 1, 0, 4) st(s) evenly spaced—60 (60, 60, 65, 65, 70, 70) sts.

cable cuffs

Purl 1 row, knit 2 rows, purl 1 row, knit 2 rows, purl 2 rows, knit 1 row, purl 1 row.

ROW 1 (RS SET-UP ROW): p2, k6, [p4 (4, 4, 5, 5, 6, 6), k6] 5 times, p2.

ROW 2 (WS): k2, [p6, k4 (4, 5, 5, 6, 6)] 5 times, p6, k2.

ROW 3: p2, work row 3 of chart C, [p4 (4, 4, 5, 5, 6, 6), work row 3 of chart C] 2 times, [p4 (4, 4, 5, 5, 6, 6), work row 3 of chart D] 3 times, p2.

Cont as est to end of cable charts, ending with a WS row. Purl 1 row, knit 1 row, purl 2 rows, knit 1 row, purl 1 row, knit 1 row, purl 1 row. Bind off loosely.

Seam sleeves. Weave in ends. Attach buttons. Block if desired.

SWEATERS, VESTS AND COATS

Autumn and winter knits are certainly the most luscious. The days are shorter, and the evenings grow longer and darker as fall fades into genuine winter, making the fireside all the cozier. The hand-knits in this chapter are knits to warm you. The yarns are lush, thick wools, and the colors are anything but dreary. Deep rich purples, varying shades of green, lush brown sprinkled with chartreuse and magenta, and bright pinks and yellows brighten these knits. Many of the patterns are easy and knit up quickly using chunky yarns and big needles…perfect for knitting during replays of *It's a Wonderful Life*.

Projects in this section include a cardigan coat knit from lush thick-and-thin wool trimmed with two shades of heathery Peruvian wool (page 110), a brightly-hued ballet-neckline top with cables and slightly flared sleeves (page 106), a gorgeous, sumptuous bulky-knit coat with oversized lace trim and shaping at the waist (page 114), as well as two versatile vests for layering (pages 82 and 86).

BACK-TO-SCHOOL
u-neck vest

Give your I.Q. a boost when you wear this quick-knit tweedy vest on the first day of fall classes. You may not be the smartest cookie in the class, but your professor doesn't have to know it—at least not until you turn in your first essay. No matter your marks, you can at least play the part of an eager-beaver learner in this scholarly vest.

Worked from the hem up to the shoulders, this vest uses a stitch pattern and darts to shape the waist and bust. Ribbing ends just below the bust where a tweedy broken-rib stitch pattern begins. The front and back are worked separately and joined at the shoulders. Trim at armhole and neckline edges is picked up and knit after the garment is complete.

finished measurements
BUST: 34 (35½, 37, 39, 41, 42½, 44, 46)"
86 (90, 94, 99, 104, 108, 112, 117)cm

yarn
3 (3, 3, 3, 3, 4, 4, 4) skeins (220 yards ea) Cascade Yarns 220 Quattro 100% wool yarn in color #9455 Turquoise Heather

needles
size US 7 (4.5mm) 24" or 29" (61 or 74cm) circular needle

size US 5 (3.75mm) 16" (41cm) circular needle

If necessary, change needle size to obtain correct gauge.

notions
stitch markers

removable markers or small safety pins

stitch holders or scrap yarn

darning needle

gauge
18 sts and 28 rows = 4" (10cm) in Waffle Stitch on larger needle

NOTES

[ ] (repeat operation): Rep the bracketed operation the number of times indicated.

in patt (in pattern): Cont to work in pattern as est.

work 2 tog (knit or purl 2 together): Dec 1 st by knitting or purling 2 sts tog as one, in keeping with est patt.

waffle stitch

Work Waffle Stitch over a multiple of 2 sts.

worked in the rnd:

RNDS 1–2: Knit.

RND 3: [k1, p1] around.

Rep Rnds 1–3.

worked flat:

ROW 1: Knit.

ROW 2: Purl.

ROW 3: [k1, p1] to end.

ROW 4: Purl.

ROW 5: Knit.

ROW 6: [p1, k1] to end.

Rep Rows 1–6.

body

With larger needle, cast on 128 (136, 144, 152, 160, 168, 176, 184) sts, place marker and join for working in the rnd, taking care not to twist sts.

Purl 3 rnds, knit 3 rnds, purl 3 rnds, knit 1 more rnd. Work in p2, k2 ribbing until piece measures 8½ (9, 9, 9½, 9½, 9½, 10, 10)" 22 (23, 23, 24, 24, 24, 25, 25)cm from cast-on edge. Purl 3 rnds, knit 3 rnds, purl 3 rnds.

NEXT RND: Remove beg of rnd marker, k1, replace marker, k64 (68, 72, 76, 80, 84, 88, 92), place second marker for right side, knit to end.

front dart shaping

NEXT RND: Work in Waffle Stitch, placing a removable marker in the 15th (16th, 17th, 18th, 19th, 20th, 21st, 22nd) st and in the 50th (53rd, 56th, 59th, 62nd, 65th, 68th, 71st) st.

Work 2 rnds even.

NEXT RND: [Work to marked st, RLI, knit marked st, LLI] twice, work to end—132 (140, 148, 156, 164, 172, 180, 188) sts.

Inc as est on last rnd on every foll 3rd rnd 5 times more—152 (160, 168, 176, 184, 192, 200, 208) sts. Work even until body measures 13 (13½, 13½, 14, 14, 14, 14½, 14½)" 33 (34, 34, 36, 36, 36, 37, 37)cm from cast-on edge.

divide front and back

Work to right side marker. Place rem 64 (68, 72, 76, 80, 84, 88, 92) sts for back on scrap yarn, to be worked later.

upper front

Bind off 4 (4, 4, 5, 5, 6, 6, 6) sts at beg of next 2 rows—80 (84, 88, 90, 94, 96, 100, 104) sts. Dec 1 st at beg of next 12 (12, 12, 12, 12, 14, 16, 16) rows—68 (72, 76, 78, 80, 82, 84, 88) sts. Work 7 rows even.

front neck

ROW 1 (RS): Work 46 (50, 52, 54, 54, 56, 58, 60) sts in patt. Place rem 22 (22, 24, 24, 26, 26, 26, 28) sts on a stitch holder to be worked later.

ROW 2: Bind off 28 (28, 28, 30, 28, 30, 32, 32) sts, work to end.

ROW 3: Work even.

ROW 4: Work 2 tog, work to end.

ROWS 5–8: Work even.

ROW 9: Work to last 2 sts, work 2 tog.

ROWS 10–14: Work even.

Rep Rows 4–14 twice more—16 (16, 18, 18, 20, 20, 20, 22) sts.

NEXT ROW: Work 2 tog, work to end.

NEXT ROW: Work to last 2 sts, work 2 tog—14 (14, 16, 16, 18, 18, 18, 20) sts.

Work even until armhole measures 8 (8, 8½, 8½, 9, 9, 9½, 9½)" 20 (20, 22, 22, 23, 23, 24, 24)cm. Bind off.

Rejoin yarn at neck edge and work right side to match, reversing shaping.

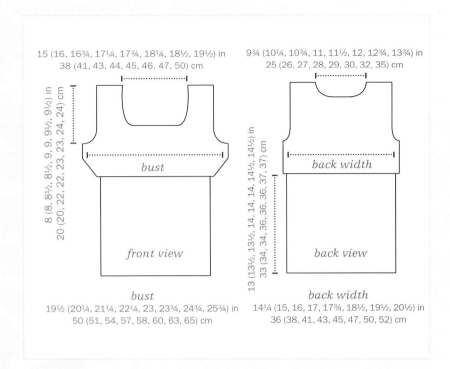

15 (16, 16¾, 17¼, 17¾, 18¼, 18½, 19½) in
38 (41, 43, 44, 45, 46, 47, 50) cm

8 (8, 8½, 8½, 9, 9, 9½, 9½) in
20 (20, 22, 22, 23, 23, 24, 24) cm

bust

front view

bust
19½ (20¼, 21¼, 22¼, 23, 23¾, 24¾, 25¾) in
50 (51, 54, 57, 58, 60, 63, 65) cm

9¾ (10¼, 10¾, 11, 11½, 12, 12¾, 13¾) in
25 (26, 27, 28, 29, 30, 32, 35) cm

13 (13½, 13½, 14, 14, 14, 14½, 14½) in
33 (34, 34, 36, 36, 36, 37, 37) cm

back width

back view

back width
14¼ (15, 16, 17, 17¾, 18½, 19½, 20½) in
36 (38, 41, 43, 45, 47, 50, 52) cm

upper back

Join yarn with RS facing. Bind off 4 (4, 4, 5, 5, 6, 6, 6) sts at beg of next 2 rows—56 (60, 64, 66, 70, 72, 76, 80) sts. Dec 1 st at each end of next 5 (6, 7, 7, 8, 9, 9, 9) rows—44 (46, 48, 50, 52, 54, 58, 62) sts. Work even until armholes measure 6 (6, 6½, 6½, 7, 7, 7½, 7½)" 15 (15, 17, 17, 18, 18, 19, 19)cm, ending with a WS row.

back neck

ROW 1 (RS): Work 27 (27, 29, 29, 31, 31, 31, 33) sts, place rem 17 (17, 19, 19, 21, 21, 21, 23) sts on stitch holder to be worked later.

ROW 2: Bind off 10 sts, work to end.

ROW 3: Work even.

ROW 4: Work 2 tog, work to end.

Rep Rows 3–4 twice more—14 (14, 16, 16, 18, 18, 18, 20) sts. Work even until armhole measures same as front. Bind off.

Rejoin yarn at neck edge and work left side to match, reversing shaping.

finishing

Seam shoulders.

neck band

With RS facing and using smaller needle, pick up and knit 3 sts for every 4 rows around neckline and join for working in the rnd. Purl 3 rnds, knit 3 rnds, purl 3 rnds. Bind off loosely.

Rep for each armhole.

Weave in ends. Block if desired.

PERFECT PERIWINKLE
turtleneck tube vest

Add a bit of sexy sophistication to your wardrobe with this turtleneck vest. Layer it over a short- or long-sleeved tee, or be daring and wear it alone for a dressed-up occasion. The form-fitting shaping and dramatically deep armholes make this piece a showstopper whether worn layered or alone.

This turtleneck is cast on at the neckline and knit in one piece to the shoulder, then split to work the armholes, and rejoined to knit the body in the round. It is truly one piece, with no additional stitches to pick up. It's knit from Cascade 220, a very soft, cozy, traditional worsted weight wool yarn.

finished measurements
BUST: 34 (36, 38, 40, 42)"
86 (91, 97, 102, 107)cm

yarn
2 (3, 3, 3, 4) skeins (220 yards ea)
Cascade Yarns 220 100% wool yarn in color 7809 periwinkle

needles
size US 7 (4.5mm) 29" (74cm) circular needle

size US 5 (3.75mm) 16" (41cm) circular needle

If necessary, change needle size to obtain correct gauge.

notions
stitch markers

stitch holders or scrap yarn

gauge
20 sts and 28 rows = 4" (10cm) in St st on larger needle

NOTES

[ ] (repeat operation): Rep the bracketed operation the number of times indicated.

sl (slip st[s] or marker): Slip a st or sts purlwise from the left needle to the right needle. Slip a marker from the left needle to the right needle, knitting the sts before and after it as usual.

KFB (knit 1 front and back): Inc 1 st by knitting into the front and back of the next st.

SSK (slip, slip, knit): Dec 1 st by slipping 2 sts knitwise one at a time, inserting tip of left needle into both sts and knitting the 2 sts tog.

M1 (make 1): Inc 1 st by picking up the bar between the next st and the st just knit and knitting into it.

RLI (right lifted increase): Inc 1 st in next st by inserting tip of right needle into back of st 1 row below on left needle and knitting into it to create a right-leaning inc.

LLI (left lifted increase): Inc 1 st in next st by inserting tip of left needle into back of st 1 row below on right needle and knitting into it.

backward loop cast on method: Holding the knitting in your right hand, and with sts on the right needle, hold the working end of the yarn in your left hand and make a loop. Twist the loop one time, so the loop is "backward," and slip it onto the right needle. Inc 1 st.

turtleneck

With smaller needle, cast on 108 (114, 114, 120, 120) sts. Place marker and join for working in the rnd, taking care not to twist sts. Work in p3, k3 rib for 5" (13cm). Change to larger needle.

divide back and front

Bind off 12 (12, 12, 15, 15) sts. Work ribbing patt over next 12 sts, k18 (21, 21, 21, 21), work ribbing for 12 sts, bind off 12 (12, 12, 15, 15) sts, work ribbing patt over 12 sts, k18 (21, 21, 21, 21), work ribbing for 12 sts. Place 42 sts onto a stitch holder or length of scrap yarn to be worked later. Work rem 42 front sts straight.

front

ROW 1 (RS): sl 1, k2, p3, k3, p3, k1, LLI, knit to last 13 sts, RLI, k1, [p3, k3] twice—44 (47, 47, 47, 47) sts.

ROW 2 (WS): sl 1, p2, k3, p3, k3, purl to last 12 sts, [k3, p3] twice.

Rep Rows 1–2 15 (16, 19, 21, 24) times more, then work Row 1 once more—76 (81, 87, 91, 97) sts. Place front sts on a length of scrap yarn.

back

Replace held sts on needle and work as for front, leaving sts on needle at end of raglan shaping.

lower body

With the back sts on needle and RS facing, use the backward loop method to cast on 9 sts. Place the front sts on the opposite end of the circular needle, making sure the RS of the fabric is facing out. Work across the front, maintaining the 12 ribbed sts at each end. Cast on 9 sts, place marker, and join for working in the rnd—170 (180, 192, 200, 212) sts.

NEXT RND: [k3, p3] twice, k52 (57, 63, 67, 73), [p3, k3] 5 times, p3, k52 (57, 63, 67, 73), [p3, k3] 3 times, p3.

Rep last rnd until work measures 3 (3½, 3½, 4, 4)" 8 (9, 9, 10, 10)cm from underarm.

NEXT RND: [k3, p3] twice, k52 (57, 63, 67, 73), [p3, k3] 6 times, p3, k40 (45, 51, 55, 61), [p3, k3] 4 times, p3.

Rep last rnd until work measures 4 (4½, 4½, 5, 5)" 10 (11, 11, 13, 13)cm from underarm. On last rnd, dec 1 (0, 0, 1, 1) st in St st sections of both front and back—168 (180, 192, 198, 210) sts.

Change to smaller needle. Work in k3, p3 rib until work measures 13" (33cm) from underarm. Bind off loosely.

finishing

Weave in ends. Block if desired.

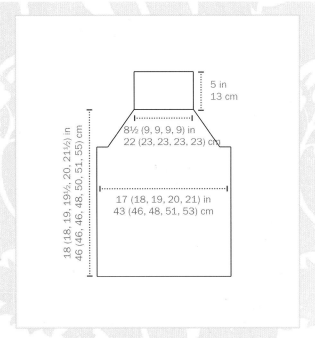

5 in
13 cm

8½ (9, 9, 9, 9) in
22 (23, 23, 23, 23) cm

18 (18, 19, 19½, 20, 21½) in
46 (46, 46, 48, 50, 51, 55) cm

17 (18, 19, 20, 21) in
43 (46, 48, 51, 53) cm

KEYHOLE-NECK BLOUSE
with eyelet details

The long silhouette of this sweater gives it a 1920s appeal, while the keyhole neckline and deep ribbing are clearly modern. Knit in this vibrant color of lightweight yarn, this sweater is great for lots of seasons. Picture yourself wearing it as you take a midnight stroll down a quiet beach in the welcome evening coolness.

Shaped using front and back darts, this long sweater is still very figure-hugging. Knit using Cascade Cotton Rich, a cotton/polyamide blend, it's soft, warm, snuggly, and it really holds its shape.

finished measurements
BUST: 30 (34, 38, 42, 46, 50, 54)"
76 (86, 97, 107, 117, 127, 137)cm

yarn
17 (19, 21, 23, 26, 28, 30) skeins (80 yards ea) Cascade Yarns Cotton Rich cotton/polyamide blend yarn in color 2151 light turquoise

needles
size US 8 (5mm) 24" or 29" (61 or 74cm) circular needle

size US 6 (4mm) 16" (40cm) circular needle

If necessary, change needle size to obtain correct gauge.

notions
stitch markers

stitch holders or scrap yarn

darning needle

one button

sewing needle and thread

gauge
16 sts and 22 rows = 4" (10cm) in St st on larger needle

NOTES

[ ] (repeat operation): Rep the bracketed operation the number of times indicated.

sl (slip st[s] or marker): Slip a st or sts purlwise from the left needle to the right needle. Slip a marker from the left needle to the right needle, knitting the sts before and after it as usual.

yo (yarn over): Wrap working yarn around needle clockwise, and knit next st as usual. This operation creates an eyelet hole in the knitting and inc 1 st.

k2tog (knit 2 together): Dec 1 st by knitting 2 sts tog.

KFB (knit 1 front and back): Inc 1 st by knitting into the front and back of the next st.

SSK (slip, slip, knit): Dec 1 st by slipping 2 sts knitwise one at a time, inserting tip of left needle into both sts and knitting the 2 sts tog.

yoke

With larger needle, cast on 58 (62, 66, 72, 76, 80, 84) sts. Do not join. Work 3 rows in St st, beg with a purl row.

RAGLAN SET-UP ROW (RS): k11 (12, 13, 14, 15, 16, 17), place marker, k7 (7, 7, 8, 8, 8, 8), place marker, k22 (24, 26, 28, 30, 32, 34), place marker, k7 (7, 7, 8, 8, 8, 8), place marker, k11 (12, 13, 14, 15, 16, 17).

Purl 1 row.

keyhole neckline and raglan shaping

NEXT ROW (RS): k2tog, [knit to marker, yo, sl marker, k1, yo] 4 times, knit to last 2 sts, SSK.

NEXT ROW: Purl.

Rep the last 2 rows 5 (5, 5, 8, 8, 8, 8) times more—94 (98, 102, 126, 130, 134, 138) sts.

NEXT ROW (RS): [Knit to marker, yo, sl marker, k1, yo] 4 times, knit to end.

NEXT ROW: Purl.

Rep the last 2 rows 5 (5, 5, 8, 8, 8, 8) times more—142 (146, 150, 198, 202, 206, 210) sts.

NEXT ROW (RS): KFB, [knit to marker, yo, sl marker, k1, yo] 4 times, knit to last st, KFB.

NEXT ROW (WS): Purl.

Rep the last 2 rows 4 (4, 4, 7, 7, 7, 7) times more, then work RS row only once more—202 (206, 210, 288, 292, 296, 300) sts. Do not turn. Join for working in the rnd.

NEXT RND: [Knit to marker, yo, sl marker, k1, yo] 4 times, knit to end.

NEXT RND: Knit.

Rep the last 2 rnds 0 (3, 6, 0, 3, 6, 9) times more—210 (238, 266, 296, 324, 352, 380) sts.

separate sleeves from body

Knit front sts, place 45 (51, 57, 64, 70, 76, 82) sts of first sleeve on scrap yarn to be worked later, place marker for left side, knit back sts, place 45 (51, 57, 64, 70, 76, 82) sts of second sleeve on scrap yarn to be worked later, place marker for right side, knit front sts—120 (136, 152, 168, 184, 200, 216) sts on needle. Consider the left side marker the beg of the rnd from now on.

body

RNDS 1–4: Knit.

RND 5: Knit to second marker, k15 (17, 19, 23, 25, 27, 29), SSK, k2tog, k22 (26, 30, 30, 34, 38, 42), SSK, k2tog, knit to end of rnd—116 (132, 148, 164, 180, 196, 212) sts.

RNDS 6–7: Knit.

RND 8: Knit to second marker, k14 (16, 18, 22, 24, 26, 28), SSK, k2tog, k20 (24, 28, 28, 32, 36, 40), SSK, k2tog, knit to end of rnd—112 (128, 144, 160, 176, 192, 208) sts.

RNDS 9–10: Knit.

RND 11: Knit to second marker, k13 (15, 17, 21, 23, 25, 27), SSK, k2tog, k18 (22, 26, 26, 30, 34, 38), SSK, k2tog, knit to end of rnd—108 (124, 140, 156, 172, 188, 204) sts.

RNDS 12–13: Knit.

RND 14: Knit to second marker, k12 (14, 16, 20, 22, 24, 26), SSK, k2tog, k16 (20, 24, 24, 28, 32, 36), SSK, k2tog, knit to end of rnd—104 (120, 136, 152, 168, 184, 200) sts.

RNDS 15–16: Knit.

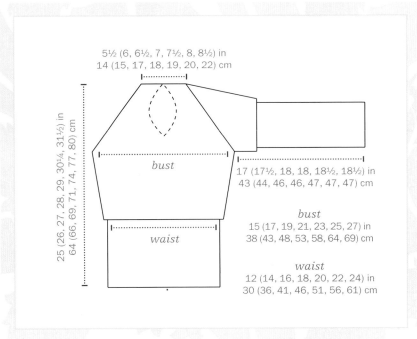

5½ (6, 6½, 7, 7½, 8, 8½) in
14 (15, 17, 18, 19, 20, 22) cm

25 (26, 27, 28, 29, 30¼, 31½) in
64 (66, 69, 71, 74, 77, 80) cm

bust

17 (17½, 18, 18, 18½, 18½) in
43 (44, 46, 46, 47, 47, 47) cm

bust
15 (17, 19, 21, 23, 25, 27) in
38 (43, 48, 53, 58, 64, 69) cm

waist

waist
12 (14, 16, 18, 20, 22, 24) in
30 (36, 41, 46, 51, 56, 61) cm

RND 17: Knit to second marker, k11 (13, 15, 19, 21, 23, 25), SSK, k2tog, k14 (18, 22, 22, 26, 30, 34), SSK, k2tog, knit to end of rnd—100 (116, 132, 148, 164, 180, 196) sts.

RNDS 18–19: Knit.

RND 20: Knit to second marker, k10 (12, 14, 18, 20, 22, 24), SSK, k2tog, k12 (16, 20, 20, 24, 28, 32), SSK, k2tog, knit to end of rnd—96 (112, 128, 144, 160, 176, 192) sts.

Work even until body measures 9" (23cm) from underarm.

bordered ribbing

Change to smaller needle. Purl 3 rnds, knit 2 rnds, purl 3 rnds, knit 2 rnds. Work in k2, p2 rib for 7" (18cm). Purl 3 rnds, knit 2 rnds, purl 3 rnds. Bind off loosely.

sleeves

Transfer the 45 (51, 57, 64, 70, 76, 82) held sts of one sleeve to larger needle. Do not join. Work 8 rows even, ending with a WS row.

NEXT ROW (RS): k22 (25, 28, 32, 35, 38, 41) sts, place marker, knit to end.

NEXT ROW: Purl.

NEXT ROW (RS): Knit to 2 sts before marker, SSK, sl marker, k2tog, knit to end.

NEXT ROW: Purl.

Rep the last 2 rows 3 times more—37 (43, 49, 56, 62, 68, 74) sts.

NEXT ROW (RS): Knit, inc 1 (3, 1, 2, 0, 2, 0) st(s) evenly spaced across—38 (46, 50, 58, 62, 70, 74) sts.

Change to smaller needle. Knit 1 row, purl 1 row, knit 2 rows, purl 2 rows, knit 2 rows, purl 1 row. Work in k2, p2 rib until

sleeve measures 16 (16½, 17, 17, 17½, 17½, 17½)" 41 (42, 43, 43, 44, 44, 44)cm from underarm, ending with a WS row. Purl 1 row, knit 1 row, purl 2 rows, knit 2 rows, purl 1 row, knit 1 row. Bind off loosely.

finishing

keyhole neck trim

With RS facing, using smaller needle, pick up and knit 12 (12, 12, 18, 18, 18, 18) sts from each of the 6 sides of the keyhole neck—72 (72, 72, 108, 108, 108, 108) sts. Place a marker at each arrow (see diagram).

ROW 1 (WS): Knit, dec 1 st at each marker—66 (66, 66, 102, 102, 102, 102) sts.

ROW 2: Purl.

ROW 3: Knit, dec 1 st at each marker—60 (60, 60, 96, 96, 96, 96) sts.

ROW 4: Purl.

ROW 5: Knit, dec 1 st at each marker—54 (54, 54, 90, 90, 90, 90) sts.

Bind off loosely.

collar trim

With RS facing and using smaller needle, pick up and knit 58 (62, 66, 72, 76, 80, 84) sts around neck. Knit 1 row, purl 1 row, knit 1 row.

NEXT ROW: k2, bind off 2 sts, knit to end.

NEXT ROW: Purl to last 2 sts, cast on 2 sts, purl to end.

Purl 1 row, knit 1 row, purl 1 row. Bind off loosely.

Seam sleeves. Weave in ends. Attach button. Block if desired.

COZY V-NECK PULLOVER
with deep ribbing

Every gal needs a stable of comfortable and classic sweaters to put into the winter-wear rotation. Even if you're sick to death of every sweater in your closet by February and you hope you never have to see one again ever, and there's still snow on the ground, I'll bet this one will still put a smile on your face when you pull it over your head.

Knit from luxurious Cascade Pastazza, this classic V-neck is a great introduction into top-down sweater construction, and it's perfect for a first sweater. This stylish essential is so versatile you'll wonder how you lived without it. Shaping is created by changing the stitch pattern.

finished measurements
BUST: 36½ (40, 43½, 48)"
93 (102, 110, 122)cm

yarn
6 (6, 7, 8) hanks (135 yards ea) Cascade Yarns Pastazza llama/wool blend yarn in color 80 brown

needles
size US 9 (5.5mm) 29" (74cm) circular needle

size US 7 (4.5mm) 29" (74cm) circular needle

If necessary, change needle size to obtain correct gauge.

notions
stitch holders or scrap yarn

stitch markers

darning needle

gauge
14 sts and 20 rows = 4" (10cm) in St st on larger needle

NOTES

[ ] (repeat operation): Rep the bracketed operation the number of times indicated.

KFB (knit 1 front and back): Inc 1 st by knitting into the front and back of the next st.

sl (slip st[s] or marker): Slip a st or sts purlwise from the left needle to the right needle. Slip a marker from the left needle to the right needle, knitting the sts before and after it as usual.

SSK (slip, slip, knit): Dec 1 st by slipping 2 sts knitwise one at a time, inserting tip of left needle into both sts and knitting the 2 sts tog.

M1 (make 1): Inc 1 st by picking up the bar between the next st and the st just knit and knitting into it.

yoke

With larger circular needle, cast on 48 sts. Do not join.

RAGLAN SET-UP ROW (WS): p1, place marker, p8, place marker, p30, place marker, p8, place marker, p1.

ROW 1 (RS): KFB, sl marker, KFB, [knit to 1 st before marker, KFB, sl marker, KFB] 3 times—56 sts.

ROW 2 AND ALL WS ROWS: Purl.

ROW 3: KFB, [knit to 1 st before marker, KFB, sl marker, KFB] 4 times, knit to last st, KFB—66 sts.

Inc as set on row 3 on every RS row 13 times more—196 sts. Join for working in the rnd.

NEXT RND: Knit.

NEXT RND: [Knit to 1 st before marker, KFB, sl marker, KFB] 4 times, knit to end—204 sts.

Rep last 2 rnds 1 (4, 7, 11) time(s) more—212 (236, 260, 292) sts. Knit 1 rnd.

separate sleeves from body

NEXT RND: Knit front sts, place 42 (48, 54, 62) sts of first sleeve on scrap yarn, knit back sts, place 42 (48, 54, 62) sts of second sleeve on scrap yarn, knit front sts—128 (140, 152, 168) sts on needle.

body

Work even for 7 (7, 8, 8)" 18 (18, 20, 20)cm. Change to smaller needle and work in k2, p2 rib until sweater measures 17 (17, 18, 18)" 43 (43, 46, 46)cm from underarm, or to desired length. Bind off loosely.

sleeves

Transfer 42 (48, 54, 62) sts for one sleeve to larger needle. Do not join. Work even in St st for 15 rows, dec 0 (2, 0, 0) sts evenly spaced on last rnd—42 (46, 54, 62) sts. Change to smaller needle. Work in k2, p2 rib until sleeve measures 18 (18, 18½, 18½)" 46 (46, 47, 47)cm from underarm, or to desired length. Bind off loosely.

finishing

With RS facing and using smaller circular needle, beg at center of V-neck, pick up and knit 21 sts along right front edge, 8 sts across top of sleeve, 30 sts across back neck, 8 sts across top of sleeve, and 21 sts along left front edge—88 sts. Do not join. Work back and forth in k2, p2 ribbing for 2" (5cm). Bind off. With yarn threaded on a darning needle, cross right flap of ribbing over left and slip st into place.

Seam sleeves. Weave in ends. Block if desired.

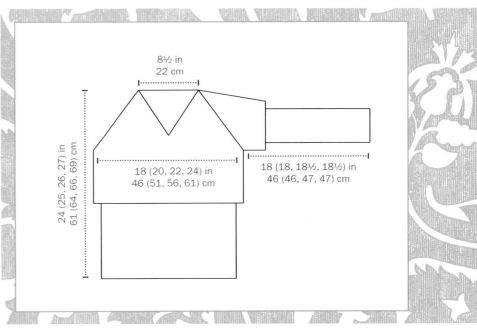

8½ in
22 cm

24 (25, 26, 27) in
61 (64, 66, 69) cm

18 (20, 22, 24) in
46 (51, 56, 61) cm

18 (18, 18½, 18½) in
46 (46, 47, 47) cm

BOATNECK BLUEBELL
sweater

Delicate and richly colored, bluebell flowers are nevertheless hearty, coming back year after year and carpeting large areas of forest. Like its namesake, this sweater combines delicate and strong features to make a decidedly feminine sweater. Corset-like shaping adds easy elegance and architectural detail to the fitted boatneck, and bold ribbed columns are repeated in the bell sleeves. It's perfect with a pair of jeans or a slim tweed skirt.

Knit using Cascade 220 tweed, this sweater is a very simple raglan pullover. Most of the shaping comes from changing the stitch pattern, though bust, back, hip and sleeve shaping are also incorporated to create a close silhouette.

finished measurements
BUST: 33 (36½, 40, 43½)"
84 (93, 102, 110)cm

yarn
5 (5, 6, 7) skeins (220 yards ea)
Cascade 220 tweed yarn in color 7606
blue tweed

needles
size US 8 (5mm) 24" or 29" (60 or
74cm) circular needle

*If necessary, change needle size to
obtain correct gauge.*

notions
stitch markers

stitch holders or scrap yarn

darning needle

gauge
18 sts and 24 rows = 4" (10cm) in
St st

NOTES

[ ] (repeat operation): Rep the bracketed operation the number of times indicated.

sl (slip st[s] or marker): Slip a st or sts purlwise from the left needle to the right needle. Slip a marker from the left needle to the right needle, knitting the sts before and after it as usual.

k2tog (knit 2 together): Dec 1 st by knitting 2 sts tog.

SSK (slip, slip, knit): Dec 1 st by slipping 2 sts knitwise one at a time, inserting tip of left needle into both sts and knitting the 2 sts tog.

KFB (knit 1 front and back): Inc 1 st by knitting into the front and back of the next st.

yoke

Cast on 108 sts, place marker and join for working in the rnd, taking care not to twist sts. Work 4 rnds garter st, beg with a knit rnd.

RAGLAN SET-UP RND: k40, place marker, k14, place marker, k40, place marker, k14.

Knit 1 rnd.

RAGLAN INC RND: [Knit to 1 st before marker, KFB, sl marker, KFB] 4 times.

Rep last 2 rnds 16 (20, 24, 28) times more—244 (276, 308, 340) sts. Knit 1 rnd.

separate sleeves from body

NEXT RND: Knit front sts, place next 48 (56, 64, 72) sts for first sleeve on scrap yarn to be worked later, place marker for left side, knit back sts, place next 48 (56, 64, 72) sts for second sleeve on scrap yarn to be worked later, place marker for right side—148 (164, 180, 196) sts on needle. Place an additional marker at center back, 37 (41, 45, 49) sts in from each side.

body

Work 5 rnds even.

RND 1: k14, SSK, k42 (50, 58, 66), k2tog, knit to 4 sts before center back marker, SSK, k4, k2tog, knit to end—144 (160, 176, 192) sts.

RND 2 AND ALL EVEN RNDS: Knit.

RND 3: k12, SSK, k44 (52, 60, 68), k2tog, knit to end—142 (158, 174, 190) sts.

RND 5: k10, SSK, k46 (54, 62, 70), k2tog, knit to 4 sts before center back marker, SSK, k4, k2tog, knit to end—138 (154, 170, 186) sts.

RND 7: k8, SSK, k48 (56, 64, 72), k2tog, knit to end—136 (152, 168, 184) sts.

RND 9: k6, SSK, k50 (58, 66, 74), k2tog, knit to 4 sts before center back marker, SSK, k4, k2tog, knit to end—132 (148, 164, 180) sts.

Work 9 rnds even. Purl 3 rnds, knit 2 rnds, purl 3 rnds, knit 2 rnds, purl 3 rnds, knit 2 rnds. Work in k2, p2 rib for 27 rnds. Knit 2 rnds, purl 3 rnds, knit 2 rnds, purl 3 rnds, knit 2 rnds, purl 3 rnds, knit 2 rnds.

hip shaping

SET-UP RND: k15, place marker, k34 (42, 50, 58) place marker, knit to end.

NEXT RND: Knit to 1 st before first front marker, KFB, sl marker, knit to second front marker, sl marker, KFB, knit to 3 sts before center back marker, KFB, k3, KFB, knit to end—136 (152, 168, 184) sts.

NEXT RND: Knit.

Rep last 2 rnds 7 times more—164 (180, 196, 212) sts. Knit 2 rnds, purl 3 rnds, knit 2 rnds, purl 3 rnds, knit 2 rnds, purl 3 rnds. Bind off.

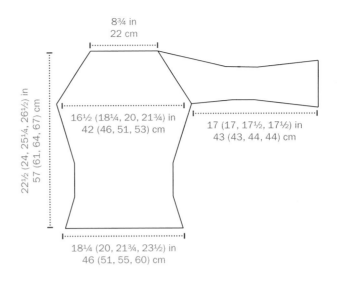

8¾ in
22 cm

22½ (24, 25¼, 26½) in
57 (61, 64, 67) cm

16½ (18¼, 20, 21¾) in
42 (46, 51, 53) cm

17 (17, 17½, 17½) in
43 (43, 44, 44) cm

18¼ (20, 21¾, 23½) in
46 (51, 55, 60) cm

sleeves

Transfer 48 (56, 64, 72) held sts of one sleeve to needle. Do not join. Work 14 rows in St st, beg with a RS row. Purl 1 row, knit 1 row, purl 2 rows, knit 2 rows, purl 1 row, knit 2 rows, purl 2 rows, knit 1 row, purl 2 rows.

NEXT ROW: Knit, dec 2 sts evenly spaced—46 (54, 62, 70) sts.

Work 11 rows in k2, p2 rib. Beg with a RS row, purl 1 row, knit 1 row, purl 2 rows, knit 2 rows, purl 1 row, knit 2 rows, purl 2 rows, knit 1 row, purl 2 rows, knit 1 row.

NEXT ROW (WS): p23 (27, 31, 35), place marker, purl to end.

NEXT ROW (RS): Knit to 2 sts before marker, KFB, k2, KFB, knit to end—48 (56, 64, 72) sts.

NEXT ROW: Purl.

Rep last 2 rows 4 times more—56 (64, 72, 80) sts. Work even in St st until sleeve measures 15½ (15½, 16, 16)" 39 (39, 41, 41)cm from underarm, ending with a WS row. Purl 1 row, knit 1 row, purl 2 rows, knit 2 rows, purl 1 row, knit 2 rows, purl 2 rows, knit 1 row, purl 2 rows, knit 1 row. Bind off.

finishing

Seam sleeves. Weave in ends. Block if desired.

TEXTURED TUNIC
with side buttons

Feeling a little zen coming on? The gently rippling stitch pattern that wraps around the bust of this tunic inspires calm in its wearer. To make the textured band, simply repeat alternating sets of knit and purl, allowing your mind to slip easily into meditative mode. An unexpected glimpse of shoulder makes this mellow tunic just the thing for a clear autumn day.

   This tunic is as simple to knit as the most basic tee. It is knit flat until the neckline is joined, and the yoke is then continued in the round. The texture at the bust, sleeve and hip add visual interest. Knit from Lana Grossa Royal Tweed, it's soft and warm and light and airy at the same time.

finished measurements
BUST: 34½ (37, 39½, 42, 44, 47)"
88 (94, 100, 107, 112, 119)cm

yarn
8 (8, 8, 9, 10, 10) balls (109 yards ea)
Lana Grossa Royal Tweed 100% wool
yarn in color 34

needles
size US 10 (6mm) 29" (74cm) circular
needle

*If necessary, change needle size to
obtain correct gauge.*

notions
removable markers or small safety pins

stitch holders or scrap yarn

darning needle

seven ¾" (2cm) buttons

sewing needle and thread

gauge
13 sts and 20 rows = 4" (10cm) in
St st

NOTES

[ ] (repeat operation): Rep the bracketed operation the number of times indicated.

sl (slip st[s] or marker): Slip a st or sts purlwise from the left needle to the right needle. Slip a marker from the left needle to the right needle, knitting the sts before and after it as usual.

KFB (knit 1 front and back): Inc 1 st by knitting into the front and back of the next st.

in patt (in pattern): Cont to work in pattern as est.

yo (yarn over): Wrap working yarn around needle clockwise, and knit next st as usual. This operation creates an eyelet hole in the knitting and inc 1 st.

work 2 tog (knit or purl 2 together): Dec 1 st by knitting or purling 2 sts tog as one, in keeping with est patt.

inc 1 (increase 1): Inc 1 st using any inc method of your choice.

seed st (seed stitch): Knit the purl sts and purl the knit sts.

box stitch

Work Box Stitch over a multiple of 4 sts.

RNDS 1–2: [k2, p2] to end.

RNDS 3–4: [p2, k2] to end.

Rep Rnds 1–4.

yoke

Cast on 80 sts. Do not join.

RAGLAN SET-UP ROW (RS): k30, place marker, k10, place marker, k30, place marker, knit to end.

NEXT ROW (WS): Purl.

RAGLAN INC ROW (RS): KFB, [knit to 1 st before marker, KFB, sl marker, KFB] 3 times, knit to last st, KFB—88 sts.

NEXT ROW (WS): Purl.

Rep last 2 rows 7 times more, then Raglan Inc Row only once more—152 sts. Do not turn. Place marker and join for working in the rnd. Knit 1 rnd.

RAGLAN INC RND: [KFB, knit to 1 st before marker, KFB, sl marker] 4 times—160 sts.

NEXT RND: Knit.

Rep last 2 rnds 3 (5, 7, 9, 11, 13) times more—184 (200, 216, 232, 248, 264) sts. Purl 3 rnds.

separate sleeves from body

NEXT RND: Knit front sts, place next 36 (40, 44, 48, 52, 56) sts for first sleeve on scrap yarn to be worked later, knit back sts, place next 36 (40, 44, 48, 52, 56) sts for second sleeve on scrap yarn to be worked later—112 (120, 128, 136, 144, 152) sts on needle. Place a removable marker in the first front st and the first back st. Consider the right underarm the beg of the rnd from now on.

body

Work in Box Stitch for 5" (13cm). Knit 1 rnd, purl 3 rnds. Work even in St st until body measures 10" (25cm) from underarm.

side slits

SET-UP RND: [Knit to marked st, purl to marked st] twice.

Cont working side slit trim at each marker for 5 more rnds, following chart from rnd 2.

divide front and back

NEXT RND: Bind off marked st, work front in patt as est, turn. Place back sts on holder to be worked later.

front hem

ROWS 1–10 AND ALL ROWS NOT OTHERWISE SPECIFIED: Work even, keeping 5 sts at each end in seed st.

ROW 11: Work 3 sts, yo, work 2 tog, work to last 4 sts, yo, work 2 tog, work 2 sts.

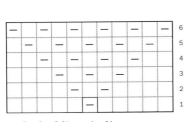

dashed lines indicate purl on RS, knit on WS.

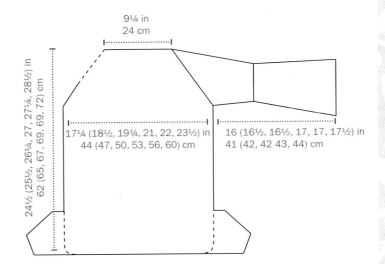

9¼ in
24 cm

24½ (25½, 26¼, 27, 27¼, 28½) in
62 (65, 67, 69, 69, 72) cm

17¼ (18½, 19¾, 21, 22, 23½) in
44 (47, 50, 53, 56, 60) cm

16 (16½, 16½, 17, 17, 17½) in
41 (42, 42 43, 44) cm

ROW 22: Rep Row 11.

ROW 33: Rep Row 11.

ROW 34: Work 2 tog, work to last 2 sts, work 2 tog.

ROW 36, 38 AND 40: Rep Row 34—47 (51, 55, 59, 63, 67) sts.

ROWS 41–47: Work 2 tog, work in seed st to end—40 (44, 48, 52, 56, 60) sts.

Bind off.

back hem

Transfer held sts to needle. With RS facing, bind off marked st, work in patt as est to end.

NOTE: Work all increased and cast-on sts into seed st patt.

ROWS 1–5 AND ALL ROWS NOT OTHERWISE SPECIFIED: Work even, keeping seed st borders at each end.

ROW 6 (RS): Work 5 sts in seed st, inc 1, place marker, knit to last 5 sts, place marker, inc 1, work 5 sts in seed st—57 (61, 65, 69, 73, 77) sts.

ROW 10 (RS): Work in seed st to marker, inc 1, sl marker, knit to marker, sl marker, inc 1, work in seed st to end—59 (63, 67, 71, 75, 79) sts.

ROW 12 (RS): Cast on 5 sts, work in seed st to marker, inc 1, sl marker, knit to marker, sl marker, inc 1, work in seed st to end, cast on 5 sts—71 (75, 79, 83, 87, 91) sts.

ROW 14 (RS): Work in seed st to marker, inc 1, sl marker, knit to marker, sl marker, inc 1, work in seed st to end—73 (77, 81, 85, 89, 93) sts.

ROWS 16, 18, 20, 22, 24, 26, 28, 30 AND 32: Rep Row 14—91 (95, 99, 103, 107, 111) sts.

ROW 34 (RS): Work 2 tog, work in seed st to marker, inc 1, sl marker, knit to marker, sl marker, inc 1, work in seed st to last 2 sts, work 2 tog.

ROWS 36, 38 AND 40: Rep Row 34.

ROWS 41–47: Work 2 tog, work in seed st to last 2 sts, work 2 tog—84 (88, 92, 96, 100, 104) sts.

Bind off.

sleeves

Transfer 36 (40, 44, 48, 52, 56) held sts of one sleeve to needle. Do not join. Knit 1 RS row.

Work 12 rows in Box Stitch, dec 1 st at beg of each row—24 (28, 32, 36, 40, 44) sts. Work even in Box Stitch for 14 rows more, ending with a WS row.

Knit 2 rows, purl 1 row, knit 1 row. Work 16 rows even in St st, inc 1 st at beg of each row—40 (44, 48, 52, 56, 60) sts. Work even in St st until sleeve measures 15 (15½, 15½, 16, 16, 16½)" 38 (39, 39, 41, 41, 42)cm from underarm. Work 8 rows in seed st. Bind off.

finishing

Seam sleeves. Weave in ends. Attach buttons. Block if desired.

ALEXANDRA
ballerina top

Not many of us can dance—or even stand—en pointe, but that doesn't mean we can't enjoy ballet-inspired fashion. Look through your drawers and closets at home, and you'll find you already have clothing with ballerina touches, from ballet slipper flats to tanks and tees gathered in a flirty V at the neckline. This feminine sweater lets you carry the airy flavor of ballet-inspired fashion into even the coldest winter months.

This sweater is worked in the round from the top down to the hem, and the sleeves are worked flat and seamed. Shaped only in the back, this sweater sports two mirrored cables on a garter stitch background in the front and one down each sleeve. The back shaping creates a subtle curve at the back hem. Knit in Lion Brand Landscapes yarn, this is a very warm knit, with lots of colorplay.

finished measurements
BUST: 34 (36, 38, 40, 42)"
86 (91, 97, 102, 107)cm

yarn
10 (11, 12, 13, 14) balls (55 yards ea) Lion Brand Landscapes wool/acrylic blend yarn in color 271 variegated blues, pinks and yellows

needles
size US 10½ (6.5mm) 24" or 29" (61 or 74cm) circular needle

If necessary, change needle size to obtain correct gauge.

notions
stitch markers

stitch holders or scrap yarn

darning needle

gauge
12 sts and 18 rows = 4" (10cm) in St st

NOTES

[ ] (repeat operation): Rep the bracketed operation the number of times indicated.

in patt (in pattern): Cont to work in pattern as est.

sl (slip st[s] or marker): Slip a st or sts purlwise from the left needle to the right needle. Slip a marker from the left needle to the right needle, knitting the sts before and after it as usual.

k2tog (knit 2 together): Dec 1 st by knitting 2 sts tog.

SSK (slip, slip, knit): Dec 1 st by slipping 2 sts knitwise one at a time, inserting tip of left needle into both sts and knitting the 2 sts tog.

KFB (knit 1 front and back): Inc 1 st by knitting into the front and back of the next st.

RLI (right lifted increase): Inc 1 st in next st by inserting tip of right needle into back of st 1 row below on left needle and knitting into it to create a right-leaning inc.

LLI (left lifted increase): Inc 1 st in next st by inserting tip of left needle into back of st 1 row below on right needle and knitting into it.

C4L (cable 4 left): Slip 2 sts to cable needle and hold to front of work. k2, k2 from cable needle.

C4R (cable 4 right): Slip 2 sts to cable needle and hold to back of work. k2, k2 from cable needle.

NOTE: Back and sleeves are worked in St st; front is worked in garter st throughout.

yoke

Cast on 76 (80, 84, 84, 92) sts, place marker and join for working in the rnd, taking care not to twist sts. Work 4 rnds garter st, beg with a knit rnd.

RAGLAN-SET UP RND: k28 (30, 32, 32, 34) sts for front, place marker, k10 (10, 10, 10, 12) sts for sleeve, place marker, k28 (30, 32, 32, 34) sts for back, place marker, k10 (10, 10, 10, 12) sts for sleeve, place marker.

CABLE SET-UP RND: KFB, p2 (3, 4, 4, 5), k8 (cable section), p6, k8 (cable section), p2 (3, 4, 4, 5), KFB, sl marker, [KFB, knit to 1 st before marker, KFB, sl marker] 3 times—84 (88, 92, 92, 100) sts.

Knit 1 rnd.

NEXT RND: KFB, purl to cable section, k8, p6, k8, purl to marker, KFB, sl marker, [KFB, knit to 1 st before marker, KFB, sl marker] 3 times—92 (96, 100, 100, 108) sts.

Rep last 2 rnds 4 times more—124 (128, 132, 132, 140) sts. Knit 1 rnd.

NEXT RND: KFB, purl to cable section, work chart A over next 8 sts beg at row 9, p6, work chart B over next 8 sts beg at row 9, purl to marker, KFB, sl marker [KFB, knit to 1 before marker, KFB, sl marker] 3 times—132 (136, 140, 140, 148) sts.

Rep last 2 rnds 6 (7, 8, 9, 9) times more—180 (192, 204, 212, 220) sts. Knit 1 rnd.

separate sleeves from body

NEXT RND: Knit front sts, place next 36 (38, 40, 42, 44) sts for first sleeve on scrap yarn to be worked later, place marker for left side, knit back sts, place next 36 (38, 40, 42, 44) sts for second sleeve on scrap yarn to be worked later, place marker for right side—108 (116, 124, 128, 132) sts on needle. Consider the right side marker the beg of the rnd from now on. Place an additional marker at center back, 27 (29, 31, 32, 33) sts in from each side seam.

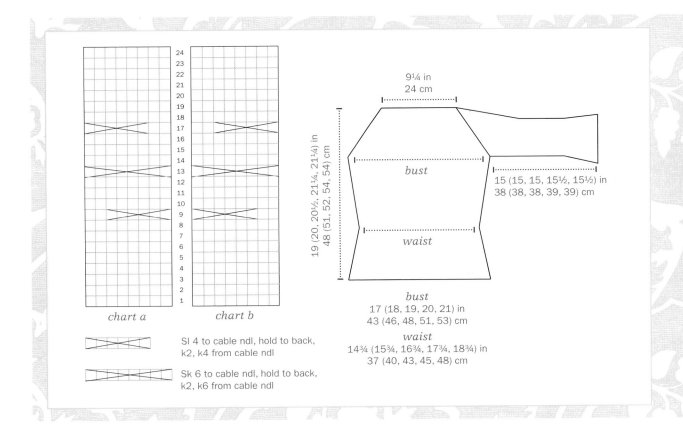

chart a

chart b

Sl 4 to cable ndl, hold to back, k2, k4 from cable ndl

Sk 6 to cable ndl, hold to back, k2, k6 from cable ndl

9¼ in
24 cm

19 (20, 20½, 21¼, 21¼) in
48 (51, 52, 54, 54) cm

bust

15 (15, 15, 15½, 15½) in
38 (38, 38, 39, 39) cm

waist

bust
17 (18, 19, 20, 21) in
43 (46, 48, 51, 53) cm

waist
14¾ (15¾, 16¾, 17¾, 18¾) in
37 (40, 43, 45, 48) cm

body

Work 7 rnds even, keeping front in garter st with cables and back in St st.

BACK DART DEC RND: Work front even, knit to 1 st before center back marker, SSK, k2, k2tog, knit to end.

Dec as est at back marker every other rnd 7 times more—92 (100, 108, 112, 116) sts rem. Work even until body measures 7½ (8, 8, 8½, 8½)" 19 (20, 20, 22, 22)cm from underarm.

BACK DART INC RND: Work front even, knit to 1 st before center back marker, RLI, k2, LLI, knit to end.

Inc as est at back marker every other rnd 7 times more—108 (116, 124, 128, 132) sts. Work 6 rnds even. Work 10 rnds garter st, beg with a knit row.Bind off loosely purlwise.

sleeves

Replace 36 (38, 40, 42, 44) sts held sts of one sleeve on needle. Do not join.

ROW 1 (RS): k18 (19, 20, 21, 22), place marker, knit to end.

ROW 2 (WS): Purl.

ROW 3: Knit to 3 sts before marker, SSK, k2, k2tog, knit to end—34 (36, 38, 40, 42) sts.

ROWS 4–6: Work even in St st.

ROW 7: Rep Row 4—32 (34, 36, 38, 40) sts.

Work even in St st until sleeve measures 4 (4, 4, 4½, 4½)" 10 (10, 10, 11, 11)cm from underarm, ending with a WS row.

CABLE SET-UP ROW (RS): k14 (15, 16, 17, 18), C4R (right sleeve) or C4L (left sleeve), k14 (15, 16, 17, 18).

NEXT ROW (WS): Purl.

NEXT ROW: k11 (12, 13, 14, 15), p1, k8, p1, k11 (12, 13, 14, 15).

NEXT ROW: p10 (11, 12, 13, 14), k2, p8, k2, p10 (11, 12, 13, 14).

NEXT ROW: k10 (11, 12, 13, 14), p2, C4R, C4L, p2, k10 (11, 12, 13, 14).

NEXT ROW: p10 (11, 12, 13, 14), k2, p8, k2, p10 (11, 12, 13, 14).

NEXT ROW: k10 (11, 12, 13, 14), p2, work row 1 of cable chart A (right sleeve) or B (left sleeve) over next 8 sts, p2, knit to end.

Work even in patt as est on last row for 33 rows more.

INC ROW (RS): Work to 1 st before p2 column, RLI, k1, p2, work cable, p2, k1, LLI, knit to end.

Inc as est on last row on every foll 4th row 3 times more—40 (42, 44, 46, 48) sts. Work 2 rows even in patt. Work 4 rows garter st. Bind off loosely.

finishing

Seam sleeves. Weave in ends. Block, stretching front to match back length.

THICK-AND-THIN
cardigan coat

Contrasting yarns, colors and textures highlight the simple construction of this stylishly oversized cardigan. The long ribbing at the hemline ensures that, even though the body is oversized and has no shaping, it still hugs those curves. A substantial cardigan is just the thing you'll reach for again and again as you pad around your house in thick, warm socks on a midwinter's eve. Or throw it on over a crisp collared shirt and stay cozy all day.

The body of the cardigan is knit with Cascade Jazz, a textural thick-and-thin wool. The cuffs, neckline and hem use Cascade 220 Heather in two complementary shades. This sweater is cast on at the neckline and knit down to the hem. Shaping is created by changing yarn, needle size and stitch pattern. The button band is picked up and knit at the end.

finished measurements
BUST: 34 (39, 44, 48)"
86 (99, 112, 123)cm

yarn
9 (10, 12, 14) balls (54 yards ea) Cascade Yarns Jazz 100% wool yarn in color 314 purple (MC)

1 (1, 2, 2) skein(s) (220 yards ea) Cascade Yarns 220 100% wool yarn in color 8267 green (CC 1); 1 (1, 2, 2) skein(s) in color 8267 (CC 2)

needles
size US 15 (10mm) 29" (74cm) circular needle

size US 7 (4.5mm) 24" or 29" (61 or 74cm) circular needle

If necessary, change needle size to obtain correct gauge.

notions
stitch markers

stitch holders or scrap yarn

darning needle

ten ¾" (2cm) buttons

sewing needle and thread

gauge
7 sts and 10 rows = 4" (10cm) in St st with MC on larger needle

NOTES

[ ] (repeat operation): Rep the bracketed operation the number of times indicated.

KFB (knit 1 front and back): Inc 1 st by knitting into the front and back of the next st.

sl (slip st[s] or marker): Slip a st or sts purlwise from the left needle to the right needle. Slip a marker from the left needle to the right needle, knitting the sts before and after it as usual.

yoke

With larger needle, cast on 40 sts. Do not join.

RAGLAN SET-UP ROW (RS): k8, place marker, k4, place marker, k16, place marker, k4, place marker, k8.

NEXT ROW (WS): Purl.

RAGLAN INC ROW: [Knit to 1 st before marker, KFB, sl marker, KFB] 4 times, knit to end—48 sts.

Rep last 2 rows 6 (8, 10, 12) times more—96 (112, 128, 144) sts. Purl 1 row.

separate sleeves from body

NEXT ROW (RS): k15 (17, 19, 21), place next 18 (22, 26, 30) sts for first sleeve on scrap yarn to be worked later, k30 (34, 38, 42) sts, place next 18 (22, 26, 30) sts for second sleeve on scrap yarn to be worked later, knit to end—60 (68, 76, 84) sts on needle.

body

Work even in St st until body measures 14" (36cm) from underarm, ending with a WS row. Change to CC 1 and smaller needle.

NEXT ROW (RS): *KFB, [knit into front, back and front again of next st] 3 times; rep from * to last 4 sts, [knit into front, back, and front again of next st] 4 times—166, 188, 210, 232 sts.

Work in k2, p2 rib for 3½" (9cm). Change to CC 2 and cont in rib for 3" (8cm) more. Bind off.

sleeves

Transfer 18 (22, 26, 30) held sts of one sleeve to larger needle. With MC, work even in St st until sleeve measures 14 (14½, 15, 15)" 36 (37, 38, 38)cm from underarm, ending with a WS row. Change to CC 1 and smaller needle.

NEXT ROW (RS): *KFB, [knit into front, back and front again of next st] 3 times; rep from * to last 2 sts, KFB twice (once, twice, once), k0 (1, 0, 1)—48 (58, 70, 80) sts.

Work in k2, p2 rib for 4" (10cm). Change to CC 2 and cont in rib for 3" (8cm) more. Bind off.

finishing

neckband

With RS facing, using smaller needle and CC 1, pick up and knit 120 sts around neck. Work in k2, p2 rib for 2" (5cm). Change to CC 2 and cont in rib for ¾" (2cm). Bind off.

button band

With RS facing, using smaller needle and CC 2, pick up and knit 156 (174, 182, 199) sts along left front edge. Knit 1 row, purl 1 row, knit 2 rows, purl 2 rows, knit 1 row, then purl 1 final row. Bind off.

buttonhole band

With RS facing, using smaller needle and CC 2, pick up and knit 156 (174, 182, 199) sts along right front edge. Knit 1 row, purl 1 row, knit 1 more row.

NEXT ROW: k5, [bind off 2 sts, k13 (15, 14, 14)] 9 (9, 10, 11) times, bind off 2 sts, knit to end.

NEXT ROW: Purl, casting on 2 sts over each bound-off section on previous row.

Purl 1 row, knit 1 row, purl 1 row. Bind off.

Seam sleeves. Weave in ends. Attach buttons. Block if desired.

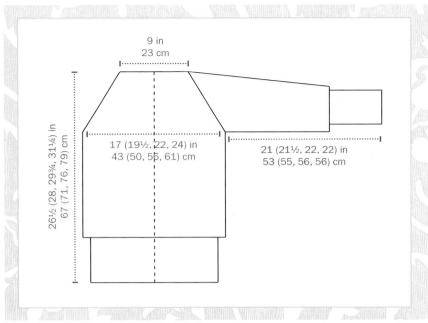

9 in
23 cm

26½ (28, 29¾, 31¼) in
67 (71, 76, 79) cm

17 (19½, 22, 24) in
43 (50, 55, 61) cm

21 (21½, 22, 22) in
53 (55, 56, 56) cm

LONG COAT
with chevron lace

When you hear the words "knit coat," your first thought is probably "eternity." However, with the right yarn and pattern you can wear your coat all winter instead of spending the season knitting it. Wrap this luscious coat around yourself as you bask in front of a cozy fire.

Knit on big needles with Cascade Tuscany Grande, you'll finish this coat in a few evenings. It's simply a raglan cardigan with bust, waist and sleeve shaping. The lace at the collar is the finishing touch, picked up after the body is knit.

finished measurements
BUST (CLOSED): 35 (39½, 43½, 48½)"
89 (100, 110, 123)cm

yarn
27 (29, 32) balls (65 yards ea) Cascade Yarns Tuscany Grande 100% wool yarn in color 40320 green

needles
size US 13 (9mm) 29" (74cm) circular needle

If necessary, change needle size to obtain correct gauge.

notions
stitch markers

stitch holders or scrap yarn

darning needle

gauge
10 sts and 13 rows = 4" (10cm) in St st

NOTES

[ ] (repeat operation): Rep the bracketed operation the number of times indicated.

sl (slip st[s] or marker): Slip a st or sts purlwise from the left needle to the right needle. Slip a marker from the left needle to the right needle, knitting the sts before and after it as usual.

KFB (knit 1 front and back): Inc 1 st by knitting into the front and back of the next st.

SSK (slip, slip, knit): Dec 1 st by slipping 2 sts knitwise one at a time, inserting tip of left needle into both sts and knitting the 2 sts tog.

k2tog (knit 2 together): Dec 1 st by knitting 2 sts tog.

in patt (in pattern): Cont to work in pattern as est.

RLI (right lifted increase): Inc 1 st in next st by inserting tip of right needle into back of st 1 row below on left needle and knitting into it to create a right-leaning inc.

LLI (left lifted increase): Inc 1 st in next st by inserting tip of left needle into back of st 1 row below on right needle and knitting into it.

yo (yarn over): Wrap working yarn around needle clockwise, and knit next st as usual. This operation creates an eyelet hole in the knitting and inc 1 st.

p2sso (pass 2 slipped sts over): Pass 2 slipped sts over the st just knit, just as for psso.

chevron lace pattern

Work the Chevron Lace Pattern over a multiple of 8 + 1 sts.

ROW 1 AND ALL WS ROWS: Purl.

ROWS 2 AND 4 (RS): k1, *SSK, [k1, yo] twice, k1, k2tog, k1; rep from * to end.

ROW 6: k1, *yo, SSK, k3, k2tog, yo, k1; rep from * to end.

ROW 8: k2, *yo, SSK, k1, k2tog, yo, k3; rep from * to end.

ROW 10: k3, *yo, sl 2, k1, p2sso, yo, k5; rep from *, end last repeat k3.

Rep Rows 1–10.

{ SIZE 35 }

yoke

With MC, cast on 30 sts.

ROW 1 (RS): k1, yo, k1, place marker, yo, k4, yo, k1, place marker, yo, k16, yo, k1, place marker, yo, k4, yo, k1, place marker, yo, k1—38 sts.

ROW 2 AND ALL EVEN ROWS (WS): Purl.

ROW 3: KFB, [knit to 1 st before marker, yo, k1, sl marker, yo] 4 times, knit to last st, KFB—48 sts.

ROWS 5, 7, 9, 11 AND 13: Rep Row 3—98 sts.

ROW 15: [Knit to 1 st before marker, yo, k1, sl marker, yo] 4 times, knit to end—106 sts.

ROW 17: Rep Row 15—114 sts.

ROW 19: Knit to 1 st before marker, yo, k1, sl marker, yo, k9, SSK, k2tog, k9, yo, k1, sl marker, yo, k15, SSK, k2tog, k15, yo, k1, sl marker, yo, k9, SSK, k2tog, k9, yo, k1, sl marker, yo, knit to end—116 sts.

separate sleeves from body

ROW 20 (WS): p18, place next 22 sts for first sleeve on scrap yarn to be worked later, p36, place next 22 sts for second sleeve on scrap yarn to be worked later, p18—72 sts on needle.

body

ROW 21: Knit.

ROW 23: k34, SSK, k2tog, k34—70 sts.

ROW 25: Knit.

ROW 27: k33, SSK, k2tog, k33—68 sts.

ROW 29: k7, SSK, k2tog, k46, SSK, k2tog, k7—64 sts.

ROW 31: k6, SSK, k2tog, k20, SSK, k2tog, k20, SSK, k2tog, k6—58 sts.

ROW 33: k5, SSK, k2tog, k40, SSK, k2tog, k5—54 sts.

ROW 35: k5, RLI, LLI, k40, RLI, LLI, k5—58 sts.

ROW 37: k6, RLI, LLI, k20, RLI, LLI, k20, RLI, LLI, k6—64 sts.

ROW 39: k7, RLI, LLI, k46, RLI, LLI, k7—68 sts.

ROW 41: Knit.

ROW 43: k33, RLI, LLI, k33—70 sts.

Work even until body measures 24" (61cm) from underarm, ending with a RS row. Work 10 rows (1 repeat) of Chevron Lace Pattern. Work 5 rows garter st. Bind off.

{ SIZE 39½ }

yoke

With MC and largest needle, cast on 38 sts.

ROW 1 (RS): k1, yo, k1, place marker, k6, yo, k1, place marker, yo, k20, yo, k1, place marker, yo, k6, yo, k1, place marker, yo, k1—46 sts.

ROW 2 AND ALL EVEN ROWS (WS): Purl.

ROW 3: KFB, [knit to 1 st before marker, yo, k1, sl marker, yo] 4 times, knit to last st, KFB—56 sts.

ROWS 5, 7, 9, 11, 13 AND 15: Rep Row 3—116 sts.

ROW 17: [Knit to 1 st before marker, yo, k1, sl marker, yo] 4 times, knit to end—124 sts.

ROW 19: Knit to 1 st before marker, yo, k1, sl marker, yo, k10, SSK, k2tog, k10, yo, k1, sl marker, yo, k17, SSK, k2tog, k17, yo, k1, sl marker, yo, k10, SSK, k2tog, k10, yo, k1, sl marker, yo, knit to end—126 sts.

ROW 21: Rep Row 17—134 sts.

ROW 23: Knit to 1 st before marker, yo, k1, sl marker, yo, k11, SSK, k2tog, k11, yo, k1, sl marker, yo, k18, SSK, k2tog, k18, yo, k1, sl marker, k1, yo, k11, SSK, k2tog, k11, yo, k1, sl marker, yo, knit to end—136 sts.

separate sleeves from body

ROW 24 (WS): p21, place next 26 sts for first sleeve on scrap yarn to be worked later, p42, place next 26 sts for second sleeve on scrap yarn to be worked later, p21—84 sts on needle.

body

ROW 25: Knit.

ROW 27: k40, SSK, k2tog, k40—82 sts.

ROW 29: k9, SSK, k2tog, k56, SSK, k2tog, k9—78 sts.

ROW 31: k8, SSK, k2tog, k25, SSK, k2tog, k25, SSK, k2tog, k8—72 sts.

ROW 33: k7, SSK, k2tog, k50, SSK, k2tog, k7—68 sts.

ROW 35: k7, RLI, LLI, k50, RLI, LLI, k7—72 sts.

ROW 37: k8, RLI, LLI, k25, RLI, LLI, k25, RLI, LLI, k8—78 sts.

ROW 39: k9, RLI, LLI, k56, RLI, LLI, k9—82 sts.

ROW 41: Knit.

ROW 43: k40, RLI, LLI, k40—84 sts.

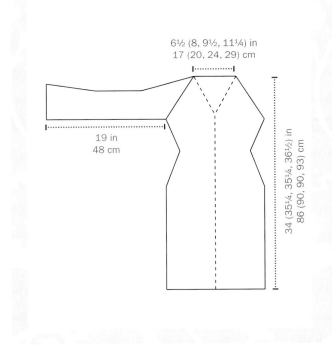

6½ (8, 9½, 11¼) in
17 (20, 24, 29) cm

19 in
48 cm

34 (35¼, 35¼, 36½) in
86 (90, 90, 93) cm

Work even until body measures 24" (61cm) from underarm, ending with a RS row. Work 10 rows (1 repeat) of Chevron Lace Pattern. Work 5 rows garter st. Bind off.

{ SIZE 43½ }

yoke

With MC and largest needle, cast on 46 sts.

ROW 1 (RS): k1, yo, k1, place marker, yo, k8, yo, k1, place marker, yo, k24, yo, k1, place marker, yo, k8, yo, k1 place marker, yo, k1—54 sts.

ROW 2 AND ALL EVEN ROWS: Purl.

ROW 3: KFB, [knit to 1 st before marker, yo, k1, sl marker, yo] 4 times, knit to last st, KFB—64 sts.

ROWS 5, 7, 9, 11, 13, 15 AND 17: Rep Row 3—134 sts.

ROW 19: KFB, knit to 1 st before marker, yo, k1, sl marker, yo, k11, SSK, k2tog, k11, yo, k1, sl marker, yo, k19, SSK, k2tog, k19, yo, k1, sl marker, yo, k11, SSK, k2tog, k11, yo, k1, sl marker, yo, knit to last st, KFB—138 sts.

ROW 21: Rep Row 3—148 sts.

ROW 23: Knit to 1 st before marker, yo, k1, sl marker, yo, k12, SSK, k2tog, k12, yo, k1, sl marker, yo, k20, SSK, k2tog, k20, yo, k1, sl marker, yo, k12, SSK, k2tog, yo, k1, sl marker, yo, knit to end—150 sts.

separate sleeves from body

ROW 24 (WS): p24, place next 28 sts for first sleeve on scrap yarn to be worked later, p46, place next 28 sts for second sleeve on scrap yarn to be worked later, p24—94 sts on needle.

body

ROW 25: Knit.

ROW 27: k45, SSK, k2tog, k45—92 sts.

ROW 29: k10, SSK, k2tog, k64, SSK, k2tog, k10—88 sts.

ROW 31: k9, SSK, k2tog, k29, SSK, k2tog, k29, SSK, k2tog, k9—82 sts.

ROW 33: K8, SSK, k2tog, k58, SSK, k2tog, k8—78 sts.

ROW 35: k8, RLI, LLI, k58, RLI, LLI, k8—82 sts.

ROW 37: k9, RLI, LLI, k29, RLI, LLI, k29, RLI, LLI, k9—88 sts.

ROW 39: k10, RLI, LLI, k64, RLI, LLI, k10—92 sts.

ROW 41: Knit.

ROW 43: k45, RLI, LLI, k45—94 sts.

Work even until body measures 24" (61cm) from underarm, ending with a RS row. Work 10 rows (1 repeat) of Chevron Lace Pattern. Work 5 rows garter st. Bind off.

yoke

With MC and largest needle, cast on 54 sts.

ROW 1 (RS): k1, yo, k1, place marker, yo, k10, yo, k1, place marker, yo, k28, yo, k1, place marker, yo, k10, yo, k1, place marker, yo, k1—62 sts.

ROW 2 AND ALL EVEN ROWS (WS): Purl.

ROW 3: KFB, [knit to 1 st before marker, yo, k1, sl marker, yo] 4 times, knit to last st, KFB—72 sts.

ROWS 5, 7, 9, 11, 13, 15, 17 AND 19: Rep Row 3—150 sts.

ROW 21: KFB, knit to 1 st before marker, yo, k1, sl marker, yo, k13, SSK, k2tog, k13, yo, k1, sl marker, yo, k22, SSK, k2tog, k22, yo, k1, sl marker, yo, k13, SSK, k2tog, k13, yo, k1, sl marker, yo, knit to last st, KFB—154 sts.

ROW 23: Rep Row 3—164 sts.

ROW 25: Knit to 1 st before marker, yo, k1, sl marker, yo, k14, SSK, k2tog, k14, yo, k1, sl marker, yo, k23, SSK, k2tog, k23, yo, k1, sl marker, yo, k14, SSK, k2tog, k14, yo, k1, sl marker, yo, knit to end—166 sts.

ROW 27: [Knit to 1 st before marker, yo, k1, sl marker, yo] 4 times, knit to end—174 sts.

separate sleeves from body

ROW 28 (WS): p27, place next 34 sts for first sleeve on scrap yarn to be worked later, p52, place next 34 sts for second sleeve on scrap yarn to be worked later, p27—106 sts on needle.

body

ROW 29: k51, SSK, k2tog, k51—104 sts.

ROW 31: k12, SSK, k2tog, k72, SSK, k2tog, k12—100 sts.

ROW 33: k11, SSK, k2tog, k33, SSK, k2tog, k33, SSK, k2tog, k11—94 sts.

ROW 35: k10, SSK, k2tog, k66, SSK, k2tog, k10—90 sts.

ROW 37: k10, RLI, LLI, k66, RLI, LLI, k10—94 sts.

ROW 39: k11, RLI, LLI, k33, RLI, LLI, k33, RLI, LLI, k11—100 sts.

ROW 41: k12, RLI, LLI, k72, RLI, LLI, k12—104 sts.

ROW 43: k51, RLI, LLI, k51—106 sts.

Work even until body measures 24" (61cm) from underarm, ending with a RS row. Work 10 rows (1 repeat) of Chevron Lace Pattern. Work 5 rows garter st. Bind off.

sleeves

Replace 22 (26, 28, 34) held sts of one sleeve on needle. Do not join.

ROW 1 (RS): k9 (11, 12, 15), SSK, k2tog, k9 (11, 12, 15)—20 (24, 26, 32) sts.

ROWS 2–20: Work even.

ROW 21 (RS): k9 (11, 12, 15), RLI, LLI, k9 (11, 12, 15)—22 (26, 28, 34) sts.

ROW 23: k10 (12, 13, 16), RLI, LLI, k10 (12, 13, 16)—24 (28, 30, 36) sts.

ROW 25: k11 (13, 14, 17), RLI, LLI, k11 (13, 14, 17)—26 (30, 32, 38) sts.

Work even until sleeve measures 15" (38cm) from underarm, ending with a WS row.

NEXT ROW (RS): Knit, inc 0 (3, 1, 3) st(s) and dec 1 (0, 0, 0) st(s) evenly spaced—25 (33, 33, 41) sts.

Work 10 rows (1 repeat) of Chevron Lace Pattern. Work 5 rows garter st. Bind off.

finishing

chevron lace at front and neck

With RS facing, beg at bottom of right front, pick up and knit 1 st for every 2 rows up right front edge, 1 st in every st around neck, and 1 st for every 2 rows down left front edge. Adjust the number of sts, if necessary, to achieve a multiple of 8 sts + 1. Work 20 rows (2 repeats) of Chevron Lace Pattern. Work 5 rows garter st. Bind off.

Seam sleeves. Weave in ends. Block if desired.

DRESS-UP CLOTHES

Sometimes you just need to look snappy, and the patterns in this section are guaranteed to make you look your best. Wearing The Saturday-in-the-Park Perfect Dress (page 130), you can't help but feel gorgeous—as if you were gloriously and perpetually frozen in the loveliest spring day. And the Tweedy V-Neck Jacket and Skirt Set (page 122) is just the thing for looking professional without sacrificing personal style.

Best of all, each of these pieces is simple and straightforward to knit. It's the small details like the faux cable swatch on the dress and the tailored lapels of the jacket that make these garments really stand out. Wear them on special occasions, or better yet, on occasions when you want to feel special.

TWEEDY V-NECK
jacket and skirt set

If you truly want to look sharp, as your mother would no doubt say you should—even if you didn't ask for her opinion—there's nothing for it but to wear a suit. Wearing this casual set knit in classic tweed, you'll be happy, and so will your mother.

The jacket is simply a V-neck cardigan with shaping at the waist. The border is picked up all around the edge after the main piece is finished. The little A-line skirt is shaped at front and back with darts, and includes a knitted-on waistband facing and hook-and-eye closures. Make your mom proud.

finished measurements

JACKET

BUST: 34 (36, 38, 40, 42)"
86 (91, 97, 102, 107)cm

SKIRT
WAIST: 24 (26, 28, 30, 32, 34, 36, 38)"
61 (66, 71, 76, 81, 86, 91, 97)cm

HIPS: 30 (32, 34, 36, 38, 40, 42 44)"
76 (81, 86, 91, 97, 102, 107, 112)cm

yarn

JACKET

5 (5, 5, 6, 6) skeins (128 yards ea) Cascade Yarns 128 Tweed 100% wool yarn in color 610 eggplant

SKIRT

3 (3, 3, 3, 3, 4, 4, 4) skeins (220 yards ea) Cascade Yarns 220 Tweed 100% wool yarn in color 7610 eggplant

needles

JACKET

size US 10½ (6.5mm) 24" or 29" (61 or 74cm) circular needle

size US 10 (6mm) 60" (150cm) circular needle

SKIRT

size US 8 (5mm) 24" or 29" (61 or 74cm) circular needle

If necessary, change needle size to obtain correct gauge.

notions

JACKET

darning needle

four 7/8" (2cm) buttons

sewing needle and thread

SKIRT

one button

two to three hook-and-eye closures

darning needle

sewing thread and sharp needle

crochet hook (optional)

gauge

JACKET

12 sts and 18 rows = 4" (10cm) in St st on larger needle

SKIRT

15 sts and 22 rows = 4" (10cm) in St st

NOTES

[ ] (repeat operation): Rep the bracketed operation the number of times indicated.

sl (slip st[s] or marker): Slip a st or sts purlwise from the left needle to the right needle. Slip a marker from the left needle to the right needle, knitting the sts before and after it as usual.

k2tog (knit 2 together): Dec 1 st by knitting 2 sts tog.

SSK (slip, slip, knit): Dec 1 st by slipping 2 sts knitwise one at a time, inserting tip of left needle into both sts and knitting the 2 sts tog.

M1 (make 1): Inc 1 st by picking up the bar between the next st and the st just knit and knitting into it.

RLI (right lifted increase): Inc 1 st in next st by inserting tip of right needle into back of st 1 row below on left needle and knitting into it to create a right-leaning inc.

LLI (left lifted increase): Inc 1 st in next st by inserting tip of left needle into back of st 1 row below on right needle and knitting into it.

JACKET

With larger needle, cast on 36 (36, 38, 38, 40) sts.

NOTE: Raglan inc, front edge inc and back dart dec are worked at the same time. Raglan inc are worked as 1 st on each side of each marker on every 2nd row, front edge inc are worked on every 5th row, and, after row 23, back dart dec are worked on every 6th row. Separate sleeve puff inc are worked on Row 16.

TO WORK RAGLAN INC: [Work to 1 st before marker, KFB, sl marker, KFB] 4 times, work to end—8 sts inc.

TO WORK FRONT INC: KFB in first and last sts of row—2 sts inc.

TO WORK BACK DART DEC: Work to 2 sts before center back marker, SSK, sl marker, k2tog, work to end.

Unless otherwise specified, purl all odd-numbered (WS) rows.

yoke

With larger needle, cast on 36 (36, 38, 38, 40) sts.

ROW 1 (WS) (RAGLAN SET-UP ROW): p2, place marker, p6, place marker, p20 (20, 22, 22, 24), place marker, p6, place marker, p2.

ROW 2 (RS): Work raglan inc—44 (44, 46, 46, 48) sts.

ROW 4: Work raglan inc—52 (52, 54, 54, 56) sts.

ROW 5: Work front inc—54 (54, 56, 56, 58) sts.

ROWS 6 AND 8: Work raglan inc—70 (70, 72, 72, 74) sts.

ROW 10: Work front inc and raglan inc—80 (80, 82, 82, 84) sts.

ROWS 12 AND 14: Work raglan inc—96 (96, 98, 98, 100) sts.

ROW 15: Work front inc—98 (98, 100, 100, 102) sts.

ROW 16 (SLEEVE PUFF INC AND RAGLAN INC): *Knit to 1 st before marker, KFB, sl marker, KFB, k2, M1, [k3, M1] 5 times, k1, KFB, sl marker, KFB; rep from * once more, knit to end—118 (118, 120, 120, 122) sts.

ROW 18: Work raglan inc—126 (126, 128, 128, 130) sts.

ROW 20: Work front inc and raglan inc—136 (136, 138, 138, 140) sts.

ROW 22: Work raglan inc—144 (144, 146, 146, 148) sts.

ROW 23 (BACK DART SET-UP ROW): p72 (72, 73, 73, 74), place marker for center back, purl to end.

ROW 24: Work raglan inc and back dart dec—150 (150, 152, 152, 154) sts.

ROW 25: Work front inc—152 (152, 154, 154, 156) sts.

ROWS 26 AND 28: Work raglan inc—168 (168, 170, 170, 172) sts.

ROW 30: Work front inc, raglan inc, and back dart dec—176 (176, 178, 178, 180) sts.

ROW 32: Work raglan inc—184 (184, 186, 186, 188) sts.

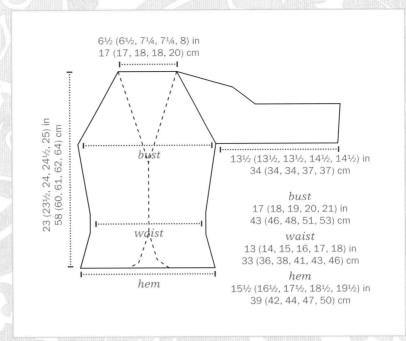

6½ (6½, 7¼, 7¼, 8) in
17 (17, 18, 18, 20) cm

23 (23½, 24, 24½, 25) in
58 (60, 61, 62, 64) cm

bust

13½ (13½, 13½, 14½, 14½) in
34 (34, 34, 37, 37) cm

bust
17 (18, 19, 20, 21) in
43 (46, 48, 51, 53) cm

waist
13 (14, 15, 16, 17, 18) in
33 (36, 38, 41, 43, 46) cm

waist

hem
15½ (16½, 17½, 18½, 19½) in
39 (42, 44, 47, 50) cm

hem

{ SIZE 34 }

Skip to Separate Sleeves from Body, below.

ROW 34: Work raglan inc—(192, 194, 194, 196) sts.

{ SIZE 36 }

Skip to Separate Sleeves from Body.

ROW 35: Work front inc—(196, 196, 198) sts.

ROW 36: Work raglan inc and back dart dec—(202, 202, 204) sts.

{ SIZE 38 }

Skip to Separate Sleeves from Body.

ROW 38: Work raglan inc—(210, 212) sts.

{ SIZE 40 }

Skip to Separate Sleeves from Body.

ROW 40: Work front inc and raglan inc—(222) sts.

{ SIZE 42 }

Cont to Separate Sleeves from Body.

separate sleeves from body

SIZE 36 ONLY: KFB, purl to marker, place next 46 sts for first sleeve on scrap yarn to be worked later, p50 back sts, place next 46 sts for second sleeve on scrap yarn to be worked later, purl to last st, KFB. Remove raglan markers, but leave center back marker in place—102 sts on needle.

{ ALL SIZES }

Purl to marker, place next 44 (–, 48, 50, 52) sts for first sleeve on scrap yarn to be worked later, p48 (–, 52, 54, 58) back sts, place next 44 (–, 48, 50, 52) sts for second sleeve on scrap yarn to be worked later, purl to end. Remove raglan markers, but leave center back marker in place—96 (–, 106, 110, 118) sts on needle.

body

Cont in St st until body measures 6" (15cm) from underarm, working front inc on every 5th row as est once more and working back dart dec on every 6th row as est 4 (4, 3, 3, 3) times more—90 (96, 102, 106, 114) sts. End with a WS row.

NEXT ROW (RS) (FRONT DART SHAPING SET-UP ROW): k12 (13, 14, 14, 15), place marker, knit to last 12 (13, 14, 14, 15) sts, place marker, knit to end.

Purl 1 row.

NEXT ROW: Knit to 2 sts before first front marker, SSK, sl marker, k2tog, knit to 2 sts before second front marker, SSK, sl marker, k2tog, knit to end—86 (92, 98, 102, 110) sts.

Work 3 rows even. Rep last 4 rows twice more—78 (84, 90, 94, 102) sts.

NEXT ROW: Knit to 1 st before first front marker, RLI, k2, LLI, knit to 1 st before center back marker, RLI, k2, LLI, knit to 1 st before second front marker, RLI, k2, LLI, knit to end—84 (90, 96, 100, 108) sts.

Work 3 rows even. Rep last 4 rows once more—90 (96, 102, 106, 114) sts.

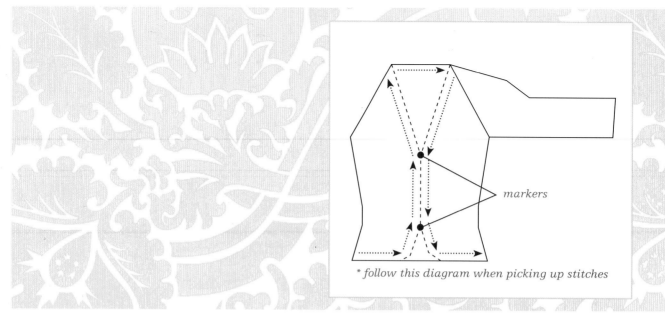

follow this diagram when picking up stitches

NEXT ROW: k2tog, knit to 1 st before first front marker, RLI, k2, LLI, knit to 1 st before center back marker, RLI, k2, LLI, knit to 1 st before second front marker, RLI, k2, LLI, knit to last 2 sts, k2tog—94 (100, 106, 110, 118) sts.

Work 3 rows even. Rep last 4 rows once more—98 (104, 110, 114, 122) sts.

NEXT ROW: k2tog, knit to last 2 sts, k2tog—96 (102, 108, 112, 120) sts.

Work 1 row even. Rep last 2 rows once more—94 (100, 106, 110, 118) sts. Do not bind off.

body trim

With RS facing, using smaller needle and beg at bottom left front, [pick up and knit 3 sts, KFB in next st] around the left front edge, back neck, and right front edge (see diagram above right), then knit rem body sts from larger needle onto trim needle. Knit to center back marker. Consider this marker the beg of the rnd from now on. Place 4 additional markers for buttonholes on left front, evenly spaced from bottom of V-neck to top of hem curve (see diagram above right).

Knit 1 rnd, then purl 3 rnds.

NEXT RND: Knit to first left front marker, [bind off 1 st, knit to next marker] 3 times, bind off 1 st, knit to end of rnd.

NEXT RND: Knit, casting on 1 st over each bound-off st of previous row.

Purl 2 rnds. Bind off purlwise using larger needle.

sleeves

Transfer 44 (46, 48, 50, 52) held sts of one sleeve to larger needle. Do not join.

ROW 1 (RS): k7 (8, 9, 10, 11), [k2tog, k3] 3 times, [SSK, k3] 3 times, knit to end—38 (40, 42, 44, 46) sts rem.

ROW 2 (WS): p19 (20, 21, 22, 23), place marker, purl to end.

ROW 3: Knit to 2 sts before marker, SSK, sl marker, k2tog, knit to end—36 (38, 40, 42, 44) sts.

Work 5 rows even, then rep Row 3 once more—34 (36, 38, 40, 42) sts.

Work even until sleeve measures 12½ (12½, 12½, 13, 13)" 32 (32, 32, 33, 33)cm from underarm, ending with a WS row.

NEXT ROW: k2tog, knit to end.

NEXT ROW: p2tog, purl to end.

Rep last 2 rows twice more—28 (30, 32, 34, 36) sts.

NEXT ROW: Knit to end, picking up and knitting 3 sts along the slanted edge.

Rep last row once more—34 (36, 38, 40, 42) sts. Purl 1 row, knit 2 rows, purl 2 rows, knit 1 more row. Bind off purlwise, using larger needle.

finishing

Seam sleeve. Weave in ends. Attach buttons. Block if desired.

SKIRT

waistband

Cast on 96 (104, 112, 120, 128, 136, 144, 152) sts. Do not join. Work 5 rows in St st, beg with a purl row. Purl 1 RS row (turning ridge). Work 10 rows in St st.

dart shaping and side seam placket

DART SET-UP ROW (WS): p10 (10, 12, 12, 15, 15, 17, 17), place left front marker, p28 (32, 32, 36, 34, 38, 40, 42), place right front marker, p20 (20, 24, 24, 30, 30, 34, 34), place right back marker, p28 (32, 32, 36, 34, 38, 40, 42), place left back marker, p10 (10, 12, 12, 15, 15, 17, 17).

DART INC ROW (RS): Knit to left back marker, M1, sl marker, knit to right back marker, sl marker, M1, knit to 1 st before right front marker, M1, k1, sl marker, k1, M1, knit to 1 st before left front marker, M1, k1, sl marker, k1, M1, knit to end.

Rep Dart Inc Row every 8th row 3 times more—120 (128, 136, 144, 152, 160, 168, 176) sts.

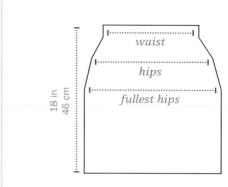

18 in / 46 cm

waist
12 (13, 14, 15, 16, 17, 18, 19) in
30 (33, 36, 38, 41, 43, 46, 48) cm

hips
15 (16, 17, 18, 19, 20, 21, 22) in
38 (41, 43, 46, 48, 51, 53, 56) cm

fullest hips
17 (18, 19, 20, 21, 22, 23, 24) in
43 (46, 48, 51, 53, 56, 58, 61) cm

skirt body

Remove dart markers. Place new marker for left side/beg of rnd and join for working in the rnd. K60 (64, 68, 72, 76, 80, 84, 88) and place marker for right side, knit to end of rnd. Work 5 rnds even.

INC RND: k1, M1, knit to 1 st before right side marker, M1, k2, M1, knit to last st, M1, k1.

Rep inc rnd every 8th rnd 3 times more—136 (144, 152, 160, 168, 176, 184, 192) sts. Work even until skirt measures 17" (43cm) from turning ridge, or desired length minus 1" (3cm).

hem

Purl 3 rnds, knit 2 rnds, then purl 3 rnds. Bind off loosely.

finishing

Fold waistband on turning ridge. With yarn threaded on a tapestry needle, slip stitch band in place on WS. With sewing needle and thread, attach hooks and eyes to placket. With yarn, make a crochet or sewn loop buttonhole on waistband edge. Attach button opposite.

Weave in ends. Block if desired.

SATURDAY-IN-THE-PARK
perfect dress

The trick to the perfect knitted dress is combining shaping with a lightweight yarn (so it keeps its shape throughout the day, and continues to flatter yours). Here I use a cotton/silk blend yarn (Cascade Pima Silk), waist and hip shaping, and a lace pattern to keep things interesting. When you wear this dress, you can't help but think of sunshine and flower-filled fields. It's like a picnic in a dress.

The dress is constructed in typical "top down raglan" fashion, cast on at the neckline, and knit in one piece to the lace-patterned hem. The textured swath around the waist and down the center of the dress looks like cables, but it's really just "mock cables" formed by combining yarn overs and passed stitches. It looks much more complex than it actually is (we knitters love that).

finished measurements
BUST: 34 (36, 38, 40, 42)"
86 (91, 97, 102, 107)cm

LENGTH FROM SHOULDER:
42½ (43¾, 44½, 45½, 46¼)"
108 (111, 113, 116, 117)cm

yarn
10 (11, 12, 12, 13) skeins (109 yards ea) Cascade Yarns Pima Silk cotton/silk blend yarn in color 5141 indigo

needles
size US 7 (4.5mm) 24" (61cm) circular needle

If necessary, change needle size to obtain correct gauge.

notions
stitch markers

stitch holders or scrap yarn

darning needle

gauge
19 sts and 24 rows = 4" (10cm) in St st

NOTES

[ ] (repeat operation): Rep the bracketed operation the number of times indicated.

sl (slip st[s] or marker): Slip a st or sts purlwise from the left needle to the right needle. Slip a marker from the left needle to the right needle, knitting the sts before and after it as usual.

SSK (slip, slip, knit): Dec 1 st by slipping 2 sts knitwise one at a time, inserting tip of left needle into both sts and knitting the 2 sts tog.

M1 (make 1): Inc 1 st by picking up the bar between the next st and the st just knit and knitting into it.

in patt (in pattern): Cont to work in pattern as est.

k2tog (knit 2 together): Dec 1 st by knitting 2 sts tog.

psso (pass slipped stitch over): Insert the tip of the left needle into the slipped st(s) on the right needle and slide it onto the left needle, bringing it over any knitted st(s) to dec.

mock cable pattern

On panel, pattern is worked over a multiple of 5 + 2 sts.

RNDS 1–2: p2, [k3, p2] to end.

RND 3: p2, [sl 1, k1, yo, k1, psso, p2] to end.

RND 4: P2, (k3, p2) to end.

Overall pattern worked in the round is worked over a multiple of 5 sts.

RNDS 1–2: [p2, k3] to end.

RND 3: [p2, sl 1, k1, yo, k1, psso] to end.

RND 4: [p2, k3] to end.

Overall pattern worked back and forth is worked over a multiple of 5 +2 sts.

ROW 1 (RS): p2, [k3, p2] to end.

ROW 2 (WS): k2, [p3, k2] to end.

ROW 3: p2, [sl 1, k1, yo, k1, psso, p2] to end.

ROW 4: k2, [p3, k2] to end.

yoke

Cast on 52 sts. Do not join.

RAGLAN SET-UP ROW (RS): k1, place marker, k10, place marker, k30, place marker, k10, place marker, k1.

NEXT ROW (WS): Purl.

RAGLAN INC ROW: [Knit to 1 st before marker, KFB, sl marker, KFB] 4 times, knit to end—60 sts.

Rep last 2 rows 24 (27, 29, 32, 34) times more—252 (276, 292, 316, 332) sts.

separate sleeves from body

NEXT ROW (WS): Purl to marker, place next 60 (66, 70, 76, 80) sts for first sleeve on scrap yarn to be worked later, purl to marker, place next 60 (66, 70, 76, 80) sts for second sleeve on scrap yarn to be worked later, purl to end—132 (144, 152, 164, 172) sts on needle.

body

Work 9 rows even, ending with a RS row. Do not turn. Place marker, cast on 27 sts onto right hand needle and join for working in the rnd—159 (171, 179, 191, 199) sts. Consider the marker the beg of the rnd from now on.

NEXT RND: Work Mock Cable Pattern over the 27 cast-on sts, knit to end.

Cont as est, with Mock Cable Pattern worked in 27-st panel at center front, until dress measures 9" (23cm) from underarm. Work 1 more rnd, adjust st count by dec 0 (1, 0, 1, 0) st/inc 1 (0, 1, 0, 1) st in St st portion of rnd—160 (170, 180, 190, 200) sts.

NEXT RND: Work Mock Cable Pattern across entire rnd.

Cont as est, working Mock Cable Pattern over all sts, until dress measures 16" (41cm) from underarm.

NEXT RND: Work Mock Cable Pattern over center 27 sts, k11 (14, 16, 19, 21) place marker (left front), k15, place marker (left side), k15, place marker (left back), k51 (55, 61, 65, 71) place marker (right back), k15, place marker (right side), k15, place marker (right front), knit to end.

hip shaping

NOTE: Cont working the center cable pattern all the way to hem.

INC RND: Work to left back marker, sl marker, M1, work to right back marker, M1, sl marker, knit to end.

NEXT RND: Work even.

Rep the last 2 rnds 3 times more—168 (178, 188, 198, 208) sts.

skirt shaping

NEXT RND: Work to 1 st before left side marker, M1, k2, M1, knit to 1 st before right side marker, M1, k2, M1, knit to end.

Work 6 rnds even. Rep last 7 rnds twice more—180 (190, 200, 210, 220) sts. Work even until dress measures 25½" (65cm) from underarm.

NEXT RND: [Work to 1 st before marker, M1, k2, M1] 6 times, knit to end.

Work 9 rnds even. Rep last 10 rnds twice more—216 (226, 236, 246, 256) sts.

hem

NOTE: Discontinue the center cable pattern here. Purl 1 rnd, knit 1 rnd.

NEXT RND: k1, [k3, yo, k2tog] around.

Knit 1 rnd, purl 1 rnd, knit 2 rnds, purl 1 rnd, knit 1 rnd.

NEXT RND: k1, [k3, yo, k2tog] around.

Knit 1 rnd, purl 1 rnd, knit 4 rnds. Rep the last 16 rnds once more. Purl 1 rnd (turning ridge). Knit 5 rnds. Bind off loosely.

sleeves

Transfer 60 (66, 70, 76, 80) held sts of one sleeve to needle. Do not join.

NEXT ROW (RS): Knit, inc 2 (1, 2, 1, 2) sts evenly spaced across—62 (67, 72, 77, 82) sts.

Purl 1 WS row.

NEXT ROW: Work Mock Cable Pattern over all sts.

Cont in patt as est for 2" (5cm). Bind off loosely.

finishing

Seam sleeves. Fold skirt hem to WS on turning ridge. With yarn threaded on a darning needle, slip st into place.

neck trim

With RS facing and beg at back right raglan line, pick up and knit 5 sts for every 6 rows around front neck and 1 st for every st along sleeves and back neck. Adjust st count if necessary to achieve a multiple of 5 + 3. Place markers at corners of front neckline, and at right and left back raglan lines.

RND 1: Purl.

RND 2: Knit, dec 1 st each side of each marker as foll: SSK, sl marker, k2tog—8 sts dec.

RND 3: [k3, yo, k2tog] to end.

RND 4: Rep rnd 2.

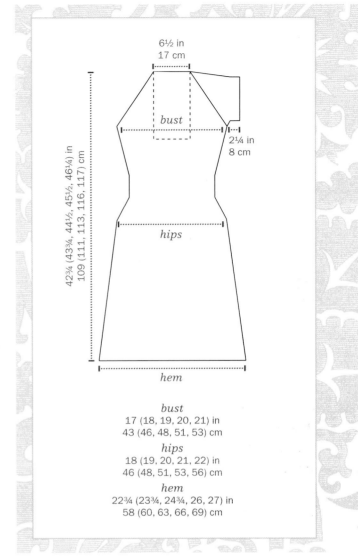

6½ in
17 cm

bust

2¼ in
8 cm

42¾ (43¾, 44½, 45½, 46¼) in
109 (111, 113, 116, 117) cm

hips

hem

bust
17 (18, 19, 20, 21) in
43 (46, 48, 51, 53) cm

hips
18 (19, 20, 21, 22) in
46 (48, 51, 53, 56) cm

hem
22¾ (23¾, 24¾, 26, 27) in
58 (60, 63, 66, 69) cm

RND 5: Purl.

RND 6: Rep Rnd 2.

RND 7: Knit.

RND 8: Purl (turning ridge).

RND 9: Knit, inc 1 st each side of each marker—8 sts inc.

RND 10: Knit.

RND 11: Rep Rnd 9.

RND 12: Knit.

RND 13: Rep Rnd 9.

Bind off loosely.

Fold hem at turning ridge and slip st into place. Weave in ends. Block if desired.

ESSENTIAL INFORMATION

Knitting Abbreviations

beg	BEGINNING	p	PURL
C4L	CABLE 4 LEFT	p2tog	PURL 2 TOGETHER
C4R	CABLE 4 RIGHT	p3tog	PURL 3 TOGETHER
CC	CONTRAST COLOR	psso	PASS SLIPPED STITCH OVER
cn	CABLE NEEDLE	rem	REMAINING
dec	DECREASE	RLI	RIGHT LIFTED INCREASE
DPN(s)	DOUBLE-POINTED NEEDLE(S)	RS	RIGHT SIDE
foll	FOLLOWING	rep	REPEAT
inc	INCREASE	sl	SLIP
k	KNIT	SKP	SLIP, KNIT, PASS
KFB	KNIT 1 FRONT AND BACK	SK2P	SLIP 2, KNIT 2 TOGETHER, PASS SLIPPED STITCH OVER
k2tog	KNIT 2 TOGETHER	SSK	SLIP, SLIP, KNIT
k3tog	KNIT 3 TOGETHER	st(s)	STITCH(ES)
LLI	LEFT LIFTED INCREASE	work 2 tog	WORK 2 TOGETHER
M1	MAKE ONE	WS	WRONG SIDE
M1P	MAKE ONE PURL	yo	YARN OVER
MC	MAIN COLOR		

Knitting Needle Conversions

diameter (in mm)	US size	suggested yarn weight
2	0	LACE WEIGHT
2.25	1	LACE AND FINGERING WEIGHT
2.75	2	LACE AND FINGERING WEIGHT
3.25	3	FINGERING AND SPORT WEIGHT
3.5	4	FINGERING AND SPORT WEIGHT
3.75	5	DK AND SPORT WEIGHT
4	6	DK, SPORT AND ARAN/WORSTED WEIGHT
4.5	7	ARAN/WORSTED WEIGHT
5	8	ARAN/WORSTED AND HEAVY WORSTED WEIGHT
5.5	9	ARAN/WORSTED, HEAVY WORSTED AND CHUNKY/BULKY
6	10	CHUNKY/BULKY
6.5	10½	CHUNKY/BULKY AND SUPER BULKY
8	11	CHUNKY/BULKY AND SUPER BULKY
9	13	SUPER BULKY
10	15	SUPER BULKY
12.75	17	SUPER BULKY
15	19	SUPER BULKY
	36	SUPER BULKY

YARN WEIGHT GUIDELINES

Since the names given to different weights of yarn can vary widely depending on the country of origin or the yarn manufacturer's preference, the Craft Yarn Council of America has put together a standard yarn weight system to impose a bit of order on the sometimes unruly yarn labels. Look for a picture of a skein of yarn with a number 1–6 on most kinds of yarn to figure out its "official" weight. Gauge is given over Stockinette stitch. The information in the chart below is taken from www.yarnstandards.com.

SUPER BULKY (6)	BULKY (5)	MEDIUM (4)	LIGHT (3)	FINE (2)	SUPERFINE (1)
bulky, roving	chunky, craft, rug	worsted, afghan, aran	dk, light, worsted	sport, baby	sock, fingering, baby
6–11 sts	12–15 sts	16–20 sts	21–24 sts	23–26 sts	27–32 sts
11 and larger	9 to 11	7 to 9	5 to 7	3 to 5	1 to 3

substituting yarns

If you substitute yarn, be sure to select a yarn of the same weight as the yarn recommended for the project. Even after checking that the recommended gauge on the yarn you plan to substitute is the same as for the yarn listed in the pattern, make sure to swatch and see. Use the chart above as a general guideline for selecting a yarn to substitute.

FINISHING

seams

Many of the patterns in this book are knitted in the round to avoid seams. Generally, however, at least a small section (or sections) of the garment does need to be seamed together. You may choose any method of seaming that works best for you or that you are familiar with. See the Reference Library (page 138) to find books that can guide you if you're new to seaming your knitted garments. Some of the best ways to seam include mattress stitch and Kitchener stitch.

To seam finished knitted pieces together with mattress stitch, simply thread a darning needle with a piece of the yarn used to knit the garment (or use a leftover tail) and stitch in and out of the stitches along each edge. Kitchener stitch is grafting live stitches together. Instead of binding off or using a permanent cast on, you leave the last stitches on a holder or on a needle and use a provisional cast on to begin the piece. Then use a darning needle to link the live stitches together, pulling them off their needles as they are secured. You may also whipstitch knitted pieces together. All seams should be worked from the right side of the knitted piece.

weaving in ends

Once your knitted piece is fully seamed together, turn it inside out and use a crochet hook or a darning needle to weave the ends in for a clean, secure finish. A crochet hook works well for weaving in short ends. If you plan to use a darning needle, make sure to leave long enough tails to easily thread through the needle. Cut off each yarn tail close to the last stitch it is woven under.

blocking

Blocking can really improve the look of your finished piece. If your stitches are uneven or your knitting looks rumpled, blocking smooths out the stitchwork. Knitted lace benefits from blocking because it opens up the delicate stitches. Blocking pieces before seaming them together can sometimes make finishing easier. If your project looks even and smooth before blocking, then you can probably skip this step because it won't affect the look of your finished piece very much.

To block knitting, pin it flat with blocking pins to folded towels or a blocking board, then spray it with water. Allow the pieces to dry fully before removing the pins. (It is important not to pin your knitting too taut or the sides of the knitting will pull in as it dries.) I don't recommend using an iron to block because the heat and pressure can flatten stitches and compromise the texture and hand of natural fibers. For a quick fix, you can hold a steam iron several inches above the pinned-out pieces and steam them gently. Do not let the iron touch the surface of the knitting. Steaming can relax and even out the stitches, but it doesn't usually work quite as well as blocking.

CARING FOR HANDKNITS

cleaning

Wash handknits in cool water using a gentle detergent. Rinse well. Never twist or wring your knits, as this will stretch the yarns and can make it difficult to reshape the garments. Rather, squeeze out as much water as you can, then roll the knits into an absorbent towel. Then stand on the towel to remove as much water as the towel can absorb. Repeat this step using dry towels until no more water seeps to the outside of the towel. Always lay handknit garments flat to dry.

storing

Store your handknits folded in a clean, dry place. When storing woolens, make sure to keep them away from moths. Cedar chips and lavender sachets help to repel moths. Keeping garments in plastic zipper bags or airtight containers also keeps knits safe from moths. Never hang your handknits.

REFERENCE LIBRARY

In my "other life," I'm a scientist. Perhaps it's because of this training that, for me, learning to knit was as much about reading and researching as it was about actual hands-on knitting time. I definitely spend much, much, much more time knitting than reading about knitting, but I honestly feel they are equally important. All knitters who hope to knit garments they actually love and wear (or even remotely like) should have a good reference library. Here you'll find a bibliography of books that I've found helpful in my personal learning process. A library doesn't have to include hundreds of books, and I think it takes a lot of looking around to even realize which books are important to own. The list of essentials is different for every knitter.

These are the books that I reach for again and again when designing my own sweaters, or when I come across a new knitting term or technique and want to learn more about it. There are a few different stitch pattern books, some purely reference and how-to books, and some knitting history books.

ELIZABETH ZIMMERMANN

You won't get too far in the knitting world without running into Elizabeth Zimmermann. Stock up on one or all four of these classic titles, and you'll instantly answer many of knitting's burning questions.

Knitter's Almanac
by Elizabeth Zimmermann

A good knitting library features all of Elizabeth Zimmermann's books (and even her videos, if you like). This one features knitting for all seasons—classic projects to keep a knitter busy throughout an entire year.

Knitting Around
by Elizabeth Zimmermann

Another classic Elizabeth Zimmermann book, this one is great for branching out into designing your own knits. Plus you'll find more of Zimmermann's own story as well as images of her knitted work and her watercolor paintings.

Knitting Without Tears
by Elizabeth Zimmermann

This classic knitting instruction book by the sardonic and witty godmother of knitting is really a must-have for any knitter's library. You'll learn how to knit a seamless sweater in the round, and along the way you'll be enlightened and amused by Zimmermann's humor and style.

Knitting Workshop
by Elizabeth Zimmermann

Reading *Knitting Workshop* is like taking a knitting class. The book supports a series of videos that Elizabeth made, wherein she teaches the basics (casting on and knitting) and takes the knitter through what she calls "master classes." The reader learns techniques like color-pattern knitting, designing sweaters knit both in the round and flat, and even how to design one's own lace shawls.

BARBARA G. WALKER

Your knitting bookshelf will be a little healthier with Barbara G. Walker's books on it as well. Her technique book and knitting stitch treasuries are invaluable references to knitters of all levels.

Knitting from the Top
by Barbara G. Walker

The knitting from the top down techniques outlined in this book underlie the construction of most of my garments. If you're interested in applying this kind of construction to other garments, this is a great resource.

Treasury of Knitting Patterns
knitting books by Barbara G. Walker

All together, Barbara G. Walker wrote four "treasury" knitting books. Originally published in the late 1960s and early 1970s by Scribner, the books had been out of print until they were recently reissued by Schoolhouse Press. Each book gives clear written patterns and instructions accompanied by photographs for hundreds of different stitches, including knit-and-purl stitches, lacework, colorwork and cables. Each volume is a veritable knitter's encyclopedia, giving not only basic stitch information, but also clear instruction on how to add stitch designs to basic patterns to personalize each handknit piece. Every knitter could use a copy of at least one of these volumes (if not all four) on his or her shelf. These books are particularly helpful if you're at all interested in designing your own patterns, or in altering patterns as given.

MORE KNITTING BOOKS

Here are some additional knitting books to fill out your collection.

Complete Book of Knitting
by Barbara Abbey

This book is an exhaustive how-to knitting manual that thoroughly explains knitting basics, including multiple methods for casting on and binding off, as well as finishing instructions, such as blocking and lining garments. In addition to basic knitting instruction, the book features over 200 illustrated pattern stitches.

Designing Knitwear
by Deborah Newton

In this instructional book, knitwear designer Deborah Newton shares her design process with knitters who want to design their own garments. Though you may not want to replicate her style exactly, this book is a wonderful resource for learning how to approach designing original handknits. Newton emphasizes creative swatching and solid documentation as hallmarks of a good design process.

Knitting in America
by Melanie Falick

In this inspirational book, author Melanie Falick interviews some of the most influential people and places involved in American knitting. The book features interviews with such pioneering knitwear designers as Meg Swansen, Priscilla Gibson-Roberts and Norah Gaughan, each of whom contributes an original design pattern to the book. In addition, there are gorgeous photographs of studios, yarn shops, farms, festivals and museums.

The New Knitting Stitch Library: Over 300 Traditional and Innovative Stitch Patterns Illustrated in Color and Explained with Easy-to-Follow Charts
by Leslie Stanfield

This reference book showcases hundreds of stitches accompanied by clear photographs. It's a great reference for uncommon cables and lace, with very easy-to-read charts.

Nicky Epstein's Knitted Embellishments: 350 Appliqués, Borders, Cords and More! and *Knitting on the Edge: Ribs, Ruffles, Lace, Fringes, Floral, Points & Picots*
by Nicky Epstein

Nicky Epstein is the queen of embellishment. These books give patterns for edgings that include fringe, cables, lace and even roses. In addition to edgings, Nicky provides numerous uses for i-cord, such as frog closures, buttons and trims. There are even instructions for knit shapes to use as appliqués.

No Idle Hands: The Social History of American Knitting
by Anne Macdonald

This delightfully written book outlines the social history of women knitting in America through times of peace and war. Macdonald's conversational, humorous tone makes for an enjoyable read.

One-Piece Knits That Fit: How to Knit and Crochet One-Piece Garments
by Margaret Hubert

Upon reading this book, I became immediately obsessed with the notion of knitting garments all in one piece. Hubert gives instructions for garments knit side-to-side, as well as in the round. This book is a must-have guide for any knitter who wants to keep sewing to an absolute minimum.

ONLINE INSPIRATION

There are lots of Web sites full of valuable information for knitters. These include online knitting dictionaries, videos to teach you to knit, chat rooms to discuss particular knitting issues, online knitting groups and clubs, and of course, free knitting patterns! Here are just a few of my favorites. There are really too many excellent knitting blogs to list them all here.

Knitting at About.com
www.knitting.about.com/
You'll find tons of free knitting patterns, stitch dictionaries and tips in this almost inexhaustible reference and resource Web site.

Knitting Techniques
www.dnt-inc.com/barhtmls/knittech.html
Find super-helpful animated knitting lessons on this Web site, for everything from short row wraps to increases and picking up stitches.

Standards and Guidelines for Crochet and Knitting
www.yarnstandards.com/index.html
Thanks to the efforts of the Craft Yarn Council of America for providing standard sizes for everything from body measurements to yarn weight to needle size. Most yarn manufacturers and pattern publishers adhere to these standards, so it's easier for knitters to find the right materials and get the right results.

Incompetech.com
www.incompetech.com/beta/plainGraphPaper/
Check out this Web site to get free knitters' graph paper. The handy calculator lets you input the size of paper you want, the spacing of the horizontal and vertical lines of the grid, and even the color of the grid lines. It then generates a PDF of your graph paper for you to print out.

Craftster.org
http://craftster.org/
Get lost in this huge online crafting forum. You never know what you'll find here—anything goes. It might just be an entirely-crocheted Jack Sparrow pirate doll. Or loafers painted with Andy Warhol soup cans. Check it out. You'll see.

MAGknits
www.magknits.com
This monthly online knitting magazine has lots of free patterns to choose from. It also reviews knitting products under the "news and reviews" link.

Knitty
www.knitty.com
Crammed with fabulous free patterns and helpful, knowledgeable articles about all knitterly topics, this online knitting magazine is the place to go when you're looking for a new project, or just a bit of inspiration. The magazine is updated quarterly, with the seasons.

RESOURCE GUIDE

YARNS

Cascade Yarns
P.O. Box 58168
Tukwila, WA 98138
www.cascadeyarns.com

Lion Brand Yarn
135 W. Kero Road,
Carlstadt, NJ 07072
www.lionbrand.com

Lana Grossa Yarns
Ingolstädter Straße 86
85080 Gaimersheim
Germany
www.lanagrossa.com

BUTTONS

Earthenwood Studio
P.O. Box 20002
Ferndale, MI 48220
www.earthenwoodstudio.com

INDEX

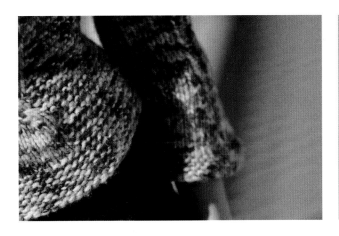

check out these other fabulous
KNITTING AND CROCHET TITLES
FROM F+W PUBLICATIONS, INC.

These books and other fine F+W Publications, Inc. titles are available at your local craft retailer, bookstore or from online suppliers.

domiKNITrix
BY JENNIFER STAFFORD

Once you know the joys of disciplined knitting, you'll never look back. Let experienced knitter Jennifer Stafford help you whip your stitches into shape. This book features a no-nonsense, comprehensive guide to essential knitting operations and finishing techniques. In the second half of the book, you'll put your knitting know-how to the test with patterns for over 20 handknit projects to wear and gift, including a halter "bra-let," a contoured zipper vest, a Jughead hat, icon sweaters and even a knitted mohawk. Plus much, much more.

ISBN-13: 978-1-58180-853-7
ISBN-10: 1-58180-853-4
FLEXIBIND CASE, 256 PAGES, Z0171

Crochet Squared
BY MARSHA A. POLK

If you can crochet a simple scarf, you can make any of the stylish and sophisticated body wraps and accessories featured in *Crochet Squared*. Each of the over 20 projects in the book is based on a simple square or rectangle shape, allowing even beginning crocheters to make gorgeous works of art. *Crochet Squared* takes crochet out of the time warp and brings it into the new millennium. Marsha Polk's striking use of color and novelty yarns makes for stunning and sophisticated projects. You'll also find a practical guide to basic crochet techniques.

ISBN-13: 978-1-58180-833-9
ISBN-10: 1-58180-833-X
PAPERBACK, 128 PAGES, 33507

Knitter's Bible: Knitted Accessories
BY CLAIRE CROMPTON

This collection of over 30 stylish knitted accessories for every season is sure to please knitters of all skill levels. Projects range from simple scarves and mittens to eye-catching hats and ponchos. With easy-to-follow techniques, detailed photography and plenty of variations, this guide is a must-have for knitters who want to create their own accessories or give a personalized gift.

ISBN-13: 978-0-7153-2327-4
ISBN-10: 0-7153-2327-X
HARDCOVER WITH CONCEALED SPIRAL, 128 PAGES, Z0465

YarnPlay
BY LISA SHOBHANA MASON

YarnPlay shows you how to fearlessly mix yarns, colors and textures to create bold and graphic handknits. You'll learn how to draw from your yarn stash to create stylish, colorful knits, including sweaters, tanks, hats, scarves, blankets, washcloths and more for women, men and children. Best of all, you'll learn knitting independence—author Lisa Shobhana Mason believes in learning the rules so you can break them. She teaches you how to take a pattern and make it your own.

ISBN-13: 978-1-58180-841-4
ISBN-10: 1-58180-841-0
PAPERBACK WITH FLAPS, 128 PAGES, Z0010